Controlled Baking

An Introduction to Controlled Small Scale
Commercial and Experimental Baking in North America

By
WULF T. DOERRY
Director, Cereal Technology
American Institute of Baking

Published by:

AMERICAN INSTITUTE OF BAKING
Manhattan, Kansas 66502

Contents

Chapter One

Chapter Two

Chapter Three

Chapter Six

Chapter Seven

Chapter Eight

Appendix A

Appendix B

Appendix C

Index

Preface

This book was written for the baking technologist who is anxious to learn the basics of baking and for the retail baker seeking new ideas and a better understanding of the craft. It also offers valuable information to the many entrepreneurs who now enter the baking trade with only a limited knowledge of the technology of baking. This book teaches the basics of product development and testing, and it discusses the various concepts of baking and ingredient technology. It also offers a variety of tested basic formulations which the reader may use for further development into new products or to improve personal skills.

This book on controlled and small scale baking is the second in a series of monographs about specific subjects in baking technology. It discusses the basic concepts of pan bread, layer cakes, creme icings and fillings, pound cake, cake muffins, cake doughnuts, and sweet dough production. It not only gives useful information about ingredients used in these various bakery foods, but it also explains how to use baker's percent and to calculate the proper amount of cake batter that can be mixed in a given size mixing bowl. This book offers many helpful hints about how to diagnose and correct faults in bakery foods and is indispensable for anyone who is interested in or responsible for product development and quality.

The author likes to thank the American Institute of

Baking for the opportunity to write this book and to test-bake the various product formulations offered as part of it. My special thanks go to Dr. James L. Vetter, AIB Vice President Technical, who encouraged me and provided the necessary time for the project. Much credit goes also to AIB Communications Director Martin Puntney who furnished some of the photography and who with his able assistant, Elizabeth Brock, converted the manuscript into this informative book. The author also thanks Anita Ricklefs for proofreading and all her helpful advice. The author's associates at AIB and his many friends in the baking and allied industries provided much appreciated assistance and arranged for the donation of many of the baking ingredients used for test-baking.

The author also thanks his family for the continued support and encouragement offered to him during his career in the baking industry which has spanned more than four decades and many different activities.

As this book goes to print, a third volume is in preparation. It will be a treatise on laminated doughs used for the manufacture of puff pastries, croissants, and Danish pastries. Even though there is much emphasis today on bakery foods with reduced calorie and fat content, the market for high quality breakfast and dessert bakery foods is still very viable and has a promising future.

Manhattan, Kansas
November 1995

CHAPTER
ONE

Experimental Baking

Experimental baking is done for either one of two reasons: to develop a new type of product, or to evaluate the performance of an ingredient. This also includes testing and optimization of new fermentation and baking technologies. Whatever the purpose, experimental baking should be done on as small a scale as possible and still remain similar to commercial production procedures.

Some laboratories have developed baking tests for specific purposes, such as determining the baking performance of new wheat varieties grown under controlled conditions. Here the availability of a very limited amount of experimentally milled flour makes it necessary to evaluate new wheat varieties from only a few grams of flour. Although micro-baking tests are very valuable for research, they are not suitable for testing the potential performance of commercial flour and of other ingredients for use in large-scale bread production.

Whatever the purpose is for experimental baking, the results are only as trustworthy as the accuracy of the baker and the capability of equipment to duplicate the conditions found in large bakery production. Also, the viability of an experimental bakery depends on the productivity of the baking technologist and the ability to reproduce test results from day to day under controlled conditions. Even though most commercial bakeries still operate under varying climatic conditions, an experimental bakery must be climatically controlled. This is not so much for the comfort of the personnel as it is to control the test parameters (conditions) so results can be compared from day to day. Also, small quantities of dough and batter are much more influenced by ambient conditions than the large amounts processed in commercial bread, cake, and sweet good bakeries.

Experimental Bakery

A well equipped experimental bakery is not only air conditioned and equipped with a desk and telephone, a mixer and an oven, but it also has adequate storage facilities for ingredients other than those which can be easily obtained from an associated production facility or from a local supplier or warehouse. Experimental bakeries should never be forced to buy ingredients in a grocery store or to procure these *as needed*! This not only takes too much time, but also prevents the experimental bakery from responding quickly to emerging needs. Also, ingredients offered in supermarkets may deviate significantly in functionality from similar ingredients used in bakeries. Because supplies and other perishable products are not used and replaced as rapidly in an experimental bakery as they are in normal manufacturing facilities, a very high standard of cleanliness is a must at all times.

Small ingredient samples should be stored in closed cabinets, where they are protected from ingredient dust, which may lead to insect infestation. Major ingredients should be stored in bins equipped with casters to facilitate cleaning of the facility. Seamless aluminum containers are ideal for keeping minor ingredients. Stainless spatulas (bowl knives) and scrapers are the basic hand tools, and no efficient bakery can operate without accurate scales and an assortment of stainless steel or aluminum bowls and pitchers. A sufficient number of various types of timers, too, is essential for avoiding costly errors in a busy shop.

Test Baking Philosophy

The purpose of experimental baking is not to produce a saleable product every time, but to study the effects of changes in formulation, processing, or ingredient performance on finished product quality. While some relatively large changes in ingredient characteristics may have only a subtle effect on product quality, a small change in the amount of a critical ingredient added to a dough or batter can have a major effect on volume and/or yeast activity. Accuracy in scaling and the availability of dependable equipment are a prerequisite for experimental baking.

All of this is wasted if the baking technologist fails to keep proper records. Good record keeping must never be sacrificed to "productivity." Good records are not only "complete" with formulations, processing parameters, observations, and measured results, but they must be presented in such a manner so that another technician not involved in this project can understand the information and replicate the experiment without additional directions from the original investigator.

If the potential for a patent application exists, all records must be permanent, i.e., in ink, dated, and signed by the record keeper and a witness. All data entries must be made in real time when the data are acquired. Important data for patent applications should never be transcribed from notes at a later time. Slightly "messy" entries are more credible than neat entries made away from the work station.

Taste Panels

In some cases, it may be desirable to employ a taste panel for sensory feedback. There are two types of taste panels: 1) trained (descriptive) taste panels, and 2) untrained (consumer) taste panels. The trained panel consists generally of a limited number of panelists (about six) trained to detect small differences in taste, flavor, texture, and mouthfeel. These differences are described by the panel members. The information developed by such a panel is very helpful for product development, especially when a product is to be duplicated or a critical ingredient is to be replaced with a substitute. A trained panel will not represent the consumer by passing judgment on the general quality of a product.

Potential acceptability of a product by consumers is best determined by larger untrained panels (preferably 15 members or more), who judge the product according to a hedonic (pleasure producing) scale. Untrained panels are more representative of the "average" consumer; but they will provide the food designer with only a limited amount of useful feedback for modifying a product.

Untrained taste panels are used for two types of tests. In the regular panel test, the members are requested to express their liking or disliking of the product on a five, seven, or nine point hedonic scale ranging from zero for "dislike very much" to "like very much" with the highest numerical score. This type of test is useful for measuring the relative preference and acceptability of several obviously different products. The number of samples evaluated by an untrained panel at any one time should be limited to not more than four, and preferably to less than four samples. This type of taste panel can also be used for the evaluation of the shelf-life of bakery products. In the shelf-life application, the panel members are asked to judge slices or small portions of bakery food for their degree of staleness.

Untrained taste panels are also used for *triangle tests*. This type of test is used for determining whether there is a noticeable difference between two products and it can only be used when all products look alike. The name comes from the fact that it uses three product samples. Two of the samples are alike and one is different (odd sample). The panel members are requested to identify the *odd sample* and to state the degree of difference between the samples, as well as which sample or samples they prefer. This type of panel, too, should consist of at least 15 members. Tables to establish the *significance* of test results are readily available from most statistical text books. For a 5% significance (probability level) at least nine of 15 panel members (60%) or 11 of 20 panelists (55%) must provide the correct answer. In a panel of 40 members only half (50%) need to be correct for the result to be significant (p = 0.05).

In order to lend validity to test panel results, all samples must be coded with random numbers. It is also recommended that panel members taste the samples in a prescribed sequence. However, this sequence must be changed in a random pattern to avoid the possibility of a lingering aftertaste from one sample always affecting the same subsequent sample. Such an error can lead to erroneous results. This is especially the case with triangle tests, in which an unchanging rotation pattern would prevent the second sample from ever becoming the "odd" sample.

Taste panel results can also be distorted when samples do not "conform" with the expectations of the panel members. The panel members must know what they are tasting. When the members taste a variation of a product that is well known and accepted by them, they tend to reject the new sample for being different from the original product, rather than accept it for its own unique qualities. For example, a company produced an excellent fruit cake. To broaden the customer base, a new variety of fruit cake was developed by the addition of almond paste to the batter. There were no other differences in the composition and appearance of the cakes. Samples of the "new" cake were given to a group of office workers, who were requested to give their hedonic (pleasure) response to the sample without being told that these samples represented a new product line. The overall response was negative because the samples did not taste like what the taste panelists had expected. However, when the panel was told what these samples actually represented and where the "different taste" came from, many of the panel members changed their minds about the samples they had rejected.

Food technologists active in product development must also be aware that sample size can influence results. When the sample size is relatively small, untrained panel members tend to prefer the sweeter samples. However, the larger the samples become, the more the panel's preference will shift to a more "neutral" taste, i.e., to a less sweet, salty, and flavored product. Always think of what the average person would consume first, a pound of very sweet cookies, or a pound of the more "neutral" potato chips or popcorn? Most people seem to agree that the rather bland chips and the popcorn will be consumed at a faster rate than the sweet cookies. In new product development it is very important that sample sizes approach the size of a normal serving.

A well designed *home-consumption test*, too, can provide the product development group with much valuable information. In this case, a selected panel member takes home a commercial-sized sample of the product and uses his/her family as a taste panel. The questionnaire passed out with each sample must allow for recorded answers from each individual family member. A trained person usually follows up such evaluations by interviewing the respondents and by making sure that the questionnaires are collected.

Bread and Roll Baking

Introduction

Although there is a very wide variety of bread and roll products available to consumers worldwide, most of the experimental baking done in North America is limited to white pan bread and hamburger buns. These two varieties represent more than half of the yeast-leavened bakery foods consumed on this continent and are, therefore, of utmost importance to the baking industry. Ingredients performing well in these two yeast-leavened baked food categories are assumed to also perform well in other varieties of bread products.

White pan bread and hamburger bun production can be easily controlled and duplicated under laboratory conditions and the criteria for their product quality are well defined. This is very important when the functionality of potential new ingredients is evaluated. The criteria for variety breads may deviate significantly from those for white pan bread.

Equipment

Although the test-baking procedures for bread and rolls should approach as closely as possible the conditions found in large-scale production, it is generally not possible to furnish an experimental bakery with equipment exactly duplicating the machinery used in industrial bakeries. A vertical 12 or 20 quart capacity three-speed mixer with a McDuffee bowl is usually substituted for large two-speed horizontal mixers used by large bread bakeries. However, a regular mixing bowl with a dough hook mixing attachment can also be used for mixing small doughs in bowls as small as 5 quarts or as large as 140 quarts.

Mechanical dough dividers and rounders are usually not found in small bakeries. Occasionally, an experimental bakery has a press divider/rounder combination available. This equipment is excellent for preparing a relatively large number of test samples. But for research and product development, individual dough pieces should be manually checked for their proper weight.

Only very few experimental and retail bakeries have the space and need for a commercial cross grain bread moulder and/or for automated roll make-up equipment. But a properly adjusted and maintained small straight grain moulder will generally suffice, even though this type of moulder will never exactly duplicate the results obtained with a cross grain moulder. To duplicate a tendercurl moulder with a small laboratory type bread moulder is virtually impossible. A small moulder can also be used to uniformly "sheet" (flatten) hamburger buns before panning.

One of the most common flaws found in loaves moulded on small straight grain moulders is a core of an open crumb structure near the center of the slices. Most of this problem is caused or aggravated by improper moulder adjustments. Unless the dough has formed a lot of gas prior to moulding, it requires only minimal sheeting prior to moulding. Tightly set degassing rollers tend to rupture the cells and cause a distinct core in the loaf. A similar adverse effect is achieved by tightening the pressure board more than necessary to seal the moulded dough piece. A loosely adjusted moulder will, in most instances, produce bread loaves with a better crumb grain than a moulder set for maximum degassing.

Moulded dough pieces for practically all pan bread produced in small and test bakeries are placed manually into bread pans. Care must be taken that the seam of the moulded loaves is at the bottom. A seam at or near the top of the loaves has an adverse effect on their symmetry.

The size of pans used for one pound white pan bread may vary from 9-10.38 inches (23-26 centimeters) in length (top inside) and from 4.38-4.5 inches (11-11.4 centimeters) in width (top inside). Their volume capacity ranges from 1600-2000 cubic centimeters. The larger pan more closely resembles what the wholesale baking industry uses. The loaves baked in these pans appear to be long and have little "break and shred" in contrast to white pan bread baked in shorter and shallower pans with a capacity of 1600 cubic centimeters. This smaller pan usually produces a larger and more visible *shred* during the early baking phase. The shred is named after the appearance of vertical gluten strands above the *break* formed when the loaf expands during the early baking phase.

While large commercial bakeries have multi-zone ovens with separate controls for each zone, most experimental and small retail bakeries are equipped with single-zone reel ovens with only a single temperature control. A few bakeries use electric deck ovens, which generally require longer baking times. Gas-fired deck ovens are also available. Wood-fired ovens are making a comeback in specialty bakeries, but have little significance in most experimental bakeries.

Rack ovens are not suitable for experimental baking, since their large baking capacity is not balanced with the limited amount of energy needed for baking product from small experimental batches. Experimental baking requires frequent opening of oven doors to check the product in the oven chamber. This tends to distort the baking conditions and makes it difficult to reproduce test results. Rack ovens are, however, successfully used by retail and in-store bakeries. Small convection ovens or ovens designed for food service kitchens are not recommended for baking test products, unless the final product is also baked in such ovens.

Test Baking of Bread and Roll Products

Experimental baking requires many judgments from the baker or baking technologist. It begins with the addition of water to form a dough from the ingredients and ends with the evaluation of the quality characteristics of the baked product. While the amount of proof (amount of expansion before baking) and the baking time and temperature can often be standardized, the amount of dough development given during mixing can vary with the flour quality and is strictly based on the baker's experience and understanding of dough characteristics.

Doughmaking Technology

Straight Dough Technology

The dough-making process inherited from the Egyptians is now called the *straight dough method*. This term implies that all ingredients for a bread dough are added *straight* to the mixer, i.e., at one time. This method does not utilize a flour preferment. In some cases salt is added after the dough is already partially mixed because it tends to interfere with the gluten development in the dough.

Except for the use of commercial yeast and optional

dough ingredients, the technology used for straight doughs today does not differ very much from that used one hundred or one thousand years ago. The wheat is now milled into refined and treated flour instead of being ground into whole meal, the water is filtered and treated, and the doughs are mixed with a mechanical mixer instead of kneaded by hand. But, in order to obtain the best quality bread by this method, the dough must still be properly conditioned either through fermentation or with *maturing agents*, such as oxidants.

The straight dough method can be used for the production of all types of bread, ranging from French bread to white pan bread and rye breads. Bakers use two slightly different straight dough methods. The traditional method utilizes a *bulk fermentation* period, during which the dough is "conditioned" by fermentation, i.e., production of fermentation acids. When the baker uses this procedure, the dough is mixed to full gluten development at 78-81° Fahrenheit (F) or 25.5-27° Celsius (C). Depending on the formulation and the amount of yeast added, straight doughs are fermented in a "warm" place (about 82-84°F or 28-29°C) for 1.5-3 hours. The baker will usually "punch" (knock down) the dough at least once after it expands to a point of maximum volume. This practice originated a long time ago when doughs were mixed by hand and yeast was scarce and expensive. The punching process added further gluten development to the dough. At the same time, the baker would "fold" the dough. This process added oxygen to the dough, which stimulated the yeast to propagate or multiply. This was very important at a time when bakers used very low yeast levels or depended on the wild yeast in their "starters."

A new type of straight dough became popular during the late 1960s. It is called the *no-time straight dough* method. This type of dough technology is the direct consequence of changing times: the advent of high-speed mechanical mixing, cheaper yeast, availability of oxidizing agents for *chemical dough development*, and increasing labor cost, i.e., a good potential for time savings. Although no-time doughs are prepared with any kind of bread mixer, they were originally promoted primarily with the use of high-speed mixers such as the Chorleywood method for the Tweedy mixer.

No-time doughs are mixed to the slightly warmer temperature of 82-84°F (28-29°C) and receive no significant bulk fermentation. They are generally transferred to the dough divider within 10-20 minutes after mixing. All further processing is the same as for other doughs. Since no-time doughs are not subjected to bulk fermentation, they do not require "degassing" prior to dividing. These doughs generally process slightly better through all make-up equipment than regular straight doughs. Since the no-time doughs are not "conditioned" by the fermentation process, this must be done through the addition of extra "maturing" (oxidizing) agents, such as 60-120 parts of ascorbic acid per million parts (ppm) of flour. Bakery ingredient suppliers offer a large selection of ingredients specifically formulated for no-time doughs. Most of these also contain L-cysteine to reduce the time it takes to develop the gluten, i.e., to mix the dough in less time.

Although shortening the dough processing time by eliminating the bulk fermentation period is of a significant advantage to the baker, the lack of fermentation has an adverse effect on the flavor and shelf-life of the baked product. While the lack of flavor is generally not much of a problem when the bread is very fresh, it is very noticeable when the no-time dough product is compared side by side with properly fermented bread, particularly after the product has staled (aged) slightly. The shelf-life of the bakery food is also adversely affected by the lack of "conditioning" through fermentation. The crumb formed during baking from a well fermented dough tends to become firm at a slower rate than the crumb from a similar dough not fermented in bulk. However, by using the proper dough oxidants (ascorbic acid and/or azodicarbonamide), dough conditioner (monocalcium phosphate and/or calcium sulfate), and, perhaps, enzymes, bread of good volume and with a good crumb texture can be produced from no-time doughs.

Sponge Dough Technology

The word *sponge* is a term having a special meaning for the baker and is not part of the definition given in a dictionary for the English language. The baker applies the term "sponge" to a preferment made from flour, water, yeast, and some minor additives which help to condition or to strengthen the flour in the dough. When this preferment is fully fermented and conditioned, its appearance somewhat resembles that of an ordinary sponge used for cleaning.

There is no rule prescribing the amount of total flour in the formula which should be prefermented. Although the percent of flour in the preferment could range from 10-100%, the baking industry in the United States usually limits this to a range of 40-80% of the total flour. As a general rule, the less "floor time" (bulk fermentation period after mixing) is given to the dough, the greater the percentage of the flour in the "sponge." Bakers who give doughs only 5-10 minutes floor time preferment 80% of the total flour in the sponge. On the other hand, bakers using only 60% of the flour in the sponge get best results when they give their freshly mixed doughs 30-45 minutes floor time, depending on the dough temperature. Bakers usually shorten the floor time slightly for doughs with a temperature above 80°F (27°C) or lengthen it for doughs cooler than desired.

The baking industry uses two types of sponges. *Plastic sponges* are generally used when more than 55% of the total flour is prefermented. Plastic sponges receive minimal mixing, just enough for the flour to absorb the water and to make sure that the yeast and other ingredients are properly distributed in the preferment. The water absorption of plastic sponges is generally limited to a range of 58-62% of the flour weight in the sponge. This amount of water gives the sponge a relatively dry and firm, or "plastic" consistency, in the unfermented stage. As fermentation proceeds, the preferment is expanded by fermentation gases and assumes a "spongy" appearance. Some bakers also call this type of sponge a *solid sponge*, to differentiate it from the second type, the *liquid sponge*.

Liquid sponges contain at least as much water as flour. The ratio of water to flour can be as high as 1.25:1.00, but is generally between 1.05 and 1.15:1.00. The limiting factor is the heat exchanger which must reduce the temperature of the fully fermented liquid sponge to slow down further yeast activity. While very "stiff" sponges are difficult to pump through plate heat exchangers, very fluid sponges may cause a problem with gluten separating from the slurry and clogging the heat exchanger plates. Although some bakers use higher or lower amounts of flour in their liquid sponges, most of them preferment about 30-50% of the total flour in the formula. Liquid sponges are generally not used by retail bakers, but may be prepared in baking laboratories, where they are chilled in an ice water bath.

Bakers tend to add all the yeast to the sponge. In liquid sponges, the yeast level is usually about 0.5% flour basis (f.b., see Appendix A, Baker's Percent) higher than the 2-2.5% (f.b.) compressed or crumbled yeast normally added to plastic sponges. Depending on ambient conditions where the fermentation is to take place, plastic sponges are generally "set" at (mixed to) a temperature of 72-77°F (22-25°C). During the cold season, the baker may prefer the warmer temperature, while during the summer, when bakeries tend to be warmer, the cooler temperatures are usually preferred. A sponge temperature of 76°F (24.5°C) is ideal for research and development work carried out in an air-conditioned baking laboratory.

The temperature of liquid preferments can be controlled more easily, and these sponges are usually "set" at slightly higher temperatures than plastic sponges. Liquid sponges formulated with less than 30% of the total flour may be started at a temperature as high as 82-84°F (28-29°C), in order to keep their total fermentation time as short as possible. Fermentation reactions are very sensitive to temperature and a difference in a few degrees can have a major impact on the time it takes for the sponge to ferment properly. Warmer preferments tend to produce off-flavors more readily than cooler sponges, thus a good control over the temperature maintained in the fermentation tanks is essential for the manufacture of high-quality bread products.

While plastic sponges are allowed to retain the heat developed during the fermentation of naturally present sugars in the dough, liquid sponges are often fermented at a specified temperature in a jacketed stainless steel tank. Sweep-wall agitation keeps the sponge at a constant temperature through heat transfer to the refrigerated cooling jacket (double wall with cavity between walls filled with a refrigerated or heated fluid for heat exchange). Therefore, liquid sponges are ideal for fully automated bakeries, which require complete control over their preferments.

Depending on the temperature and yeast level in the preferment, plastic sponges are usually fermented for three to six hours. Most bakeries, however, ferment plastic sponges for 3.5-4.5 hours. During this time, the temperature of the sponge generally rises between 7-10°F (4-5.5°C). Longer fermentation times are usually needed with low levels of yeast in the sponge. To keep the proof time at about 60 minutes, the doughs made from slowly fermented sponges are often "spiked" (boosted) at the remix stage with an additional small amount of yeast. The same is sometimes necessary for doughs made from liquid sponges.

Because liquid ferments are normally fermented at higher temperatures than plastic sponges, their fermentation time is usually slightly shorter. As a general rule, the less flour in the liquid ferment, the shorter the fermentation time and the warmer the setting (initial) temperature for the sponge. Also, when the flour in the preferment is less than 30% of the total flour in the final dough, a small amount of sugar (about one percent of the total flour weight) is usually added to the sponge to provide sufficient fermentable solids. Higher levels of sugar tend to produce more organic acids and to lower the pH of the preferment more rapidly; but when the pH in the ferment becomes very low, the high acidity starts to have an adverse effect on the crumb structure of the baked product. This potential problem does not exist in liquid sponges prepared with 40% or more of the total flour because the flour not only provides sufficient sugar for the fermentation, but it also has a very good buffering effect on the pH of the preferment.

The fermentation time for liquid sponges varies from about 1.5 hours for a very low flour content to about three hours when 50% or more of the flour is prefermented. Liquid sponges are fermented and stored in stainless steel tanks, which require significantly less floor-space than the equipment used for plastic sponges. With the development of new metering devices, liquid sponges of all densities can now be transferred quickly and accurately to mixers.

Water Brews

Water brews were very popular during the 1970s. During the 1980s bakers gradually replaced these brews with liquid sponges or they returned to using plastic sponges, provided the plant did not suffer from a severe lack of space. Although bread manufactured from water brews has a very good eye appeal, many bakers and consumers agree that it lacks a good flavor and shelf-life. Today, very few bakers still use the water brew method for manufacturing their breads.

Water brews contain less than 10% of the total flour in the dough or no flour. All the fermentable solids in the brew are added as sugar, primarily as high-fructose corn syrup. Since these water brews contain no significant amount of flour, a chemical buffer must be added to prevent the pH of the brew from dropping to such a low level that it inhibits the yeast. This chemical buffer generally consists of a blend of calcium carbonate, ammonium sulfate, and calcium sulfate. Some salt and flour or starch are often added to the buffer to dilute the mix for more accurate scaling. The baker usually formulates the water brew with about two-thirds of the total dough water (40-45% of the flour weight in the formula), about 2% f.b. sugar solids, all the yeast (about 3% f.b.), 0.5% f.b. salt, and 0.2% f.b. brew buffer. The mix is allowed to ferment for about 1.5-2 hours at 82-84°F (28-29°C), or until there is no further drop in the pH of the brew.

Since the added sugar is the only source of fermentables for the yeast, the amount of sugar in the brew has a significant effect on the final pH and on the total acid content in the brew. However, most of the acid in the brew is carbonic acid, which forms when carbon dioxide dissolves in water. Since the solubility of carbon dioxide is inversely related to the temperature, higher fermentation temperatures for water brews generally result in lower amounts of acid retained by the brew. Also, except for some sourness, carbonic acid contributes very little to the overall flavor of bread. This may have been an important factor in the decision of some bakers to abandon this breadmaking technology in favor of flour preferments.

Formulating Preferments

The major advantage of preferments over straight doughs is the added control the baker and the technologist have over the fermentation process. This added control comes from the longer fermentation time used for only part of the flour. A lower fermentation temperature and a slightly lower yeast level than used for straight doughs also add to a more controlled performance of this dough system. Liquid preferments (sponges) are not practical in small bakeries and are seldom used in experimental baking laboratories. The vast majority of bakers using preferments prefer plastic sponges for their ease of handling, even though they require more total fermentation and processing time.

When formulating plastic sponges for bread and bun doughs, the technologist and baker must keep in mind that the purpose of the preferment is to provide sufficient time for conditioning part of the flour by controlled yeast fermentation, enzymes, and with added chemical dough conditioners. For this reason, plastic sponges consist not only of more than half of the total flour (55-80%), water (58-62% of the flour weight in the sponge), and most or all of the yeast, but also of the mineral yeast food and other dough conditioners, such as flour oxidants and monocalcium phosphate (if necessary to acidify the dough).

Another purpose of the preferment is to hydrate those ingredients requiring more time for this purpose than normally available during mixing and dough processing. Coarsely ground whole wheat, cracked wheat, fiber ingredients, and wheat gluten are often added to sponges for an extended hydration time.

Although shortenings and vegetable oil are usually added at the dough remix stage, dough strengtheners and other high melting point surfactants not dispersed in water or soft fat, such as sodium stearoyl lactylate (SSL) and powdered distilled monoglycerides, should be added to the sponge for better dispersion and increased effectiveness. Mold inhibitors, salt, sugar, dairy products, and fast-acting flour oxidants should never be added to preferments.

Except for less flour (10-55% of total flour) and for more water in liquid flour ferments, the basic rules are the same for plastic and liquid preferments. Since liquid sponges are usually prepared for more than one dough at a time, and are often used for a variety of breads, the main difference between them and plastic sponges is the deletion of ingredients from the liquid sponge, which are not common in all doughs made with this preferment. High-fiber and whole wheat breads are rarely prepared from liquid sponges because they usually contain extra vital wheat gluten or whole wheat flour which are not part of most other bread doughs.

At the completion of their fermentation, the preferments contain large air cells entrapped in a glutinous web formed from the flour. At this point, the plastic sponges have expanded to maximum volume and start to "settle back" and to have a relatively flat top. They will collapse easily when they are physically disturbed. Liquid flour

Temperature controlled fermentation cabinet for preferments.

preferments will behave similarly, except that they are even more sensitive to physical disturbance. No-flour water brews have a low gas retention and will not expand noticeably during fermentation.

While liquid preferments are usually passed through a heat exchanger before their temporary storage at 41°F (5°C) in a temperature controlled tank, plastic sponges are generally processed into doughs immediately after they are properly conditioned by fermentation.

Under laboratory conditions, liquid preferments set for more than a single dough should be cooled as they would be in large commercial production. This is best done by placing the fermentation container with the ferment into a larger bowl filled with ice water. The preferment is then cooled by sweeping it slowly with a rubber spatula against the cold wall of the fermentation container until the desired storage temperature of 41°F (5°C) is reached. Liquid preferments set for single doughs may be used like plastic sponges and without prior cooling. However, if a warm preferment makes it difficult to control the dough temperature in the desired range of 78-80°F (25.5-27°C), then it is advisable to cool the liquid preferment to at least a temperature that no longer adversely affects the desired final dough temperature.

Unless compensated for in the dough stage, underfermented preferments produce bread and rolls of lower volume and with an open grain and thick cell walls. Overfermented preferments may cause an excessive loaf volume with an irregular break and a poor shred where the loaf expands during the early baking stage. Some of these symptoms may be offset with changes in the amount of oxidation added to doughs made from these under- or overfermented preferments. A slight increase in the oxidation level will generally improve the performance of underfermented sponges, while a decrease in oxidation may eliminate the "wildness" of the break and shred in bread loaves and hamburger buns made from overfermented preferments.

Controlling Dough Temperature

All ingredients not added to the sponge, including the remaining flour and water and the fast-acting flour oxidants, are added to the preferment at the dough remix stage. Unless refrigeration for the mixing bowl is available, the final dough temperature after mixing is controlled with the water temperature and with the addition of ice in place of some of the dough water.

Whenever ice is used, one should not forget that there is a difference in the cooling capacity of ice cubes removed from the freezer at -4°F (-20°C) and of shaved ice in ice water at 32°F (0°C). Ice equilibrated with water at 32°F (0°C) absorbs only the latent heat, which is the energy required to transform ice from 32°F to water at 32°F. This latent heat is equivalent to 144 BTU[a]/lb (80 cal[b]/g) and constitutes the major cooling effect of ice. Ice added at -4°F (-20°C) absorbs an additional 18 BTU/lb (10 cal/g) of heat, which increases its cooling effect by an additional 12.5%.

Dough Water Absorption

Although the *optimum dough water absorption* for a flour can only be established with a series of test-bakes, an experienced baker can estimate the amount of water to be added to bread dough by feeling the consistency (softness) of the dough. Bakeries receiving large shipments of flour can request copies of quality control rheological test data from the mill. These tests generate dough viscosity data in response to extended mixing of flour/water doughs under controlled conditions and indicate not only the flour's tolerance to mixing, but also how much water the flour absorbs for a desired dough consistency (viscosity).

The water absorption for flour reported with Farinograph (a dough rheology testing instrument, page 72 *Baking Technology, Breadmaking*, Volume 1) data is, however, only for flour/water doughs. Other ingredients in bread doughs may cause a significant deviation from this value. While most bread doughs have an optimum dough water absorption slightly greater than the Farinograph absorption, some may even have a lower absorption than

---

[a] BTU: British Thermal Unit (the energy required to raise the temperature of 1 lb. of water by 1°F)

[b] cal: Calorie (the energy required to raise the temperature of 1 g of water by 1°C)

indicated by this instrument. Fortunately, once the relationship between the Farinograph information and the actual formula absorption is established, this difference usually remains relatively constant. Generally, the information provided by the mill can serve as a valuable starting point for determining the effective dough absorption of a new flour.

Dough Mixing

The dough mixing process has three basic functions:

- Uniform blending of dough ingredients
- Hydration of flour and of other dry ingredients
- Development of gluten structure

The blending of ingredients requires physical action (energy). Although the hydration of flour initially depends on this physical blending step, it requires primarily time and little energy after the dry ingredients make contact with the liquid ingredients. This is particularly true for the coarser grain meals and some fiber ingredients. Also, cold doughs take longer to hydrate than warmer doughs. The gluten development is the most energy demanding and time consuming part of the dough mixing process, no matter what type of mixer is used for this purpose.

Mechanism of Gluten Development

In order to develop gluten from the two wheat flour proteins, glutenin and gliadin, these proteins need to be hydrated and a cohesive dough mass must be formed. Initially, the protein molecules are coiled and/or folded into a relatively compact shape. Intramolecular disulfide (-S-S-) bonds between adjacent layers or coils of the same molecule keep these molecules in this configuration until the internal bonds are broken by physical force of the mechanical mixing action or by chemical reduction (L-cysteine). As doughs are mixed and more and more of the intramolecular disulfide bonds are broken, the coils and folds in the protein molecules are stretched apart and different molecules are bonded together with new disulfide bridges. This gradual reshaping of protein molecules into a mixture of a two-dimensional film and a three-dimensional matrix makes doughs extensible and improves the gas retention of the cell structure. The baker calls this process *dough development*.

As doughs are mixed, the mixer operator can check the progress of dough development by stretching a small piece of dough into a fine film. When this film is extensible and approaches transparency without apparent lumps and veins, or irregularities in the film, the baker considers the dough "fully developed." Continued mixing will increase the dough's extensibility, but in a one-dimensional way, i.e., the dough becomes "stringy" and very sticky. Because overmixed doughs have lost elasticity, they are difficult to remove from the mixing bowl and their stickiness leads to an excessive use of "dusting flour" during processing. Since the structural and film-forming properties of overmixed doughs are impaired, the resulting loaves tend to be smaller and have an open, irregular crumb structure.

Floor Time

After the dough is mixed, it is allowed to ferment under ambient conditions, either on a flour-dusted surface, or in the mixing bowl (if it is available for this purpose). This fermentation time for the fresh dough is generally called *floor time*. The length of it varies according to how much of the flour was prefermented in the sponge. As a

Mixed dough in the McDuffee mixing bowl.

Experimental bread mixed with dough hook.

Dough pieces checked for gluten development.

rule, the more flour prefermented in the sponge, the shorter the floor time needed for the dough. This floor time may be as short as 10-15 minutes for doughs prepared from 70-80% flour sponges, or as long as 30-45 minutes when only 30-50% of the flour was prefermented. Cooler doughs (below 78°F or 25.5°C) receive usually slightly longer floor times than warmer doughs (82°F or 28°C).

Straight doughs (doughs prepared without the benefit of preferments) may receive a floor time from as little as 5 minutes (*no-time dough*) to as much as three hours (*fermented straight dough*). No-time doughs contain more yeast (3-4% f.b.) and flour oxidizing agents (ascorbic acid) than fermented straight doughs (2-3% f.b. yeast) and are usually mixed to a warmer temperature (82-84°F or 28-29°C) than the fermented straight doughs (78-80°F or 25.5-26.5°C).

Dividing the dough with a bench scraper.

When doing research or product evaluation, any abnormal dough characteristics, such as soft, stiff and dry "feel" as well as "stickiness" must be recorded and reported with other dough make-up properties.

Dividing of Dough

The vast majority of small and experimental doughs is divided and scaled manually. This is usually done with a metal scraper made from stainless steel and on a bench with a wooden or plastic top. Maple hardwood makes an excellent bench top and is no longer considered a "health hazard." Properly maintained and regularly cleaned, hardwood surfaces will not promote the propagation of pathogenic, or illness causing, bacteria. A wooden bench top should never be used for cutting or chopping food. When dough is divided on a wooden bench top, it should never be done with a "chopping" motion, but by bringing the straight

Folding of the dough piece for rounding.

Rounding the dough pieces while stretching the dough skin.

Finish rounding of a dough piece.

Intermediate proof for rounded dough pieces.

cutting edge of the scraper down level with the bench top. Hitting the wooden bench top with the corner of a scraper will soon cause severe damage to the bench's surface. Heavy soaking of wooden bench tops with water for cleaning is not recommended either. This causes the wood to swell and to form cracks upon drying. These cracks and rough bench surfaces cannot be cleaned properly and provide potential harborage for unwanted and pathogenic micro-organisms and should be repaired immediately.

Stainless steel bench tops are not recommended for processing doughs, because metal rapidly absorbs and dissipates heat from the dough and environment. Since experimental doughs are usually small, this heat loss or gain may significantly affect the fermentation process.

Rounding of Dough Pieces

When the dough pieces are *rounded* by hand, a smooth skin is formed by folding the edges of the dough piece toward its center. This process is then completed by rolling the irregular and folded portion of the dough piece in short strokes and under slight pressure between the palm of the hand and the flour-dusted bench top. By exerting the pressure away from the smooth side of the dough piece, the skin on it is stretched and a tight dough ball is produced. This dough ball is then placed on a flour-dusted surface and covered with a cloth (or a lid, if placed in a container) for a 10-15 minute intermediate proof (rest). During this time, the dough relaxes sufficiently for further processing.

The smaller dough pieces for rolls are usually rounded on a very lightly flour-dusted bench top by holding the dough pieces between the cupped hand and the bench and moving them under light pressure in a circular motion until a smooth dough ball is obtained.

A straight grain moulder

Moulding

Before the dough pieces are moulded, they are usually flattened by hand and partially degassed. The degassing process is then completed by two sets of sheeting rollers mounted on the moulding equipment. These degassing rollers have a smooth surface and are adjusted to the smallest gap possible without rupturing the dough skin. Ruptured dough may not only cause problems as "sticky" dough pieces, but will also cause a severe *core* (an open and coarse crumb structure) in parts of the bread crumb. If possible (and safe!), the dough pieces should be turned manually by 90 degrees after they emerge from the first set of sheeting rollers and before they enter the second set of degassing rolls. This turning has the same effect as achieved with a cross grain moulder.

Contrary to the belief of many bakers and technologists, an "open" crumb grain at the center of the baked loaves cannot be corrected by simply reducing the gap between the degassing rolls and lowering the pressure board on the moulding table. A "core" is more likely caused by settings which are too tight than by too much gap between the sheeting rolls and too little pressure exerted by the pressure board.

The pressure board is designed to seal together the various dough curls in the moulded loaf, but not to degas the moulded dough piece. In fact, a very tight setting of the pressure board usually has the opposite effect by causing a core or by enlarging an existing one. A very tight setting will also cause a poor loaf symmetry by shaping the dough piece into a dumbbell (thick ends and a thin middle). Often, small pieces of dough are shaved off such moulded dough pieces and are picked up again by subsequent loaves. This causes severe variations in the weight of the baked product.

On the other hand, when the dough pieces are not properly degassed, the bread tends to have an open and non-uniform grain. This is often the case with product prepared from fermented straight doughs. Also, a pressure board that exerts too little pressure during moulding may not properly fuse together the individual layers of the curled dough piece, especially when too much dusting flour is used at the same time. This usually results in an irregular cell structure in the baked product. But overall, a slightly loose pressure board will produce better results than a pressure board adjusted too tightly!

Since different types of dough (and sometimes also different flours) may require different moulder adjustments for best results, the optimum moulder settings must be verified periodically with test bakes. All moulded dough pieces should be placed into clean and glazed bread pans

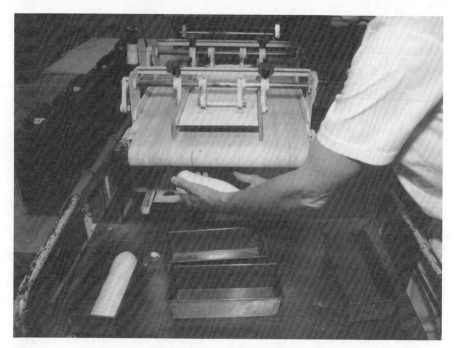

Manual panning of moulded loaves.

with the seam facing down. Identifying tags are best placed at one end of the loaf wedged between the dough piece and the pan wall, so that these test loaves can be easily recognized while they are cooling.

Moulding by Hand

There may be occasions when the baking technologist or the baker needs to mould bread loaves by hand. This is accomplished by fully degassing and flattening the dough piece either with the palm of the hand, a rolling pin, or a mechanical sheeter. The flattened dough piece is then folded in half and the two ends (about two inches) are folded towards the middle, so that the dough piece now has three straight sides and one "rounded" side. The width of this piece should now be about the same as the desired length of the moulded loaf. By folding about one third of the dough

Degassing of dough piece before moulding.

Hand moulding of dough piece.

Hand moulded dough piece.

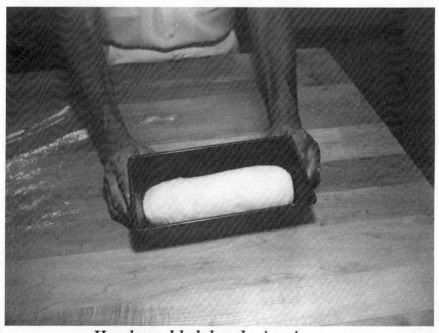

Hand moulded dough piece in pan.

piece from the straight side over towards the rounded edge and by gently sealing the folded portion to the unfolded section, the formation of air pockets is minimized. The folding and sealing steps should be repeated two or more times to complete the moulding process. Care should be taken to keep the ends of the cylindrical loaves as "square" as possible.

Baking Pans

In contrast to Europe, where much test-baking is done with hard rolls, most experimental baking in North America is done with white pan bread. There is no standard pan available for this purpose. However, if the experimental bakery is associated with a bread production facility, it is recommended that the experimental bakery use pans, formulations, and scaling weights identical to those used by the commercial plant. Although single pans are available for one-pound loaves with a capacity of 1600 and 1800 cubic centimeters (98 and 110 cubic inches), commercial bakeries usually use pans with a capacity of at least 2000 cubic centimeters (122 cubic inches). Smaller pans are more useful for research because they better show the *break and shred* of loaves, which are quite often good indicators for the proper oxidation level in the bread, as well as for other potential deficiencies.

The *break and shred* is formed near the top crust of the loaves by the rapid expansion of the bread during the early stages of baking. An even (straight-line) break without a crack and with a smooth shred is desirable. The shred consists of a series of vertical dough (gluten) strands originating from the break and ending at the top crust. The ideal shred is formed by very fine dough strands and is uniform for the entire length of the loaf. While underoxidized bread often lacks the break and shred even in the smaller pans (small loaves), overoxidized loaves tend to have a "wild" (jagged looking) break with an uneven shred. Commercial bread pans are relatively large (2000 cubic centimeters or larger) and bread baked in them usually does not exhibit a pronounced "break and shred."

Bread pans should be manufactured from tin-plated steel or from aluminized steel and they should be of the same configuration and construction as commercial bread pans. The pans should be color-treated to enhance the absorption of radiated heat, and they should be glazed for easy release of the baked product. Regular aluminum bread pans are not representative of what the baking industry uses and tend to give a slightly different bake.

Proofing

In order to be able to study the effect of ingredients and formulation on yeast activity, it is always important to accurately control temperature and humidity in the proofing cabinet that is used for the final fermentation step. The position of louvers or baffles used to control the airflow in these cabinets must be checked periodically to ensure that the temperature in the cabinet is uniform throughout. Unless the loaves and rolls are proofed for a predetermined amount of time, they must be proofed "to height," i.e., to the same degree of expansion. Most experimental bakers use a set of templates to measure the height of the expanded dough pieces above the pan. Another way to accomplish this is to measure the total height of the proofed unit in the pan with a graduated gauge.

During proofing (final fermentation period) the dough is allowed to warm up in order to accelerate the production of carbon dioxide by the yeast. This gas causes the dough to "rise" and to expand to about three times its original volume. The carbon dioxide is concentrated primarily in

Graduated gauge for measuring the proof height of bread loaves.

Loading test loaves on an oven shelf.

tiny air cells produced during dough mixing and it provides the desired *leavening* for soft bread and rolls.

This process is facilitated by a *proofer*, which is generally an enclosed room or cabinet with a controlled environment. The temperature for proofing pan bread is normally maintained in the range of 104-113°F (40-45°C). Bakers trained in Europe and those who use the same proofer for sweet rolls and Danish pastries tend to use the lower temperatures in this range. Bread bakers in the United States prefer proof temperatures at the upper end of the range because American yeast is more tolerant to higher temperatures.

The relative humidity (RH) is normally adjusted to a level which prevents the formation of a dry crust on the dough. This is usually in the range of 80-85% RH or a 5-6°F (2.8-3.3°C) differential between dry and wet bulb temperatures. The *wet bulb temperature* is obtained by keeping the "bulb" of a mercury type thermometer, or the sensing portion of a dial or electronic thermometer moistened with a wet cotton wick. Unless the air in the proofer is saturated with moisture (100% RH), the wet bulb temperature is lower than the dry bulb temperature due to the cooling effect of moisture evaporation from the cotton wick.

Most white breads and rolls are given a *full proof*. In this application the term "full" is synonymous with maximum or optimum. It means that with the additional expansion in the oven, the loaves and rolls will reach the desired maximum volume. Excessive proof opens up the crumb grain and weakens the dough structure. This may cause the overproofed loaves to collapse during their transfer to the oven. When a fully proofed loaf is lightly touched, it will offer little resistance; but it should not leave a permanent impression when the finger is removed. The dough surface should feel moist, but neither "tacky" nor wet.

Experimental 1 lb. loaves baked in 1800 cc pan (left) and 1600 cc pan (right).

Baking

The baking time and temperature are influenced by the type of oven used and depend on the oven load versus oven capacity. Bread bakes faster in convection ovens. For this reason, the temperature in convection ovens is usually set 20-30°F (11-17°C) lower than in gas fired reel ovens (ovens with self-levelling trays suspended between two revolving reels). In order to retain as much moisture as possible in the crumb, the bread and rolls should be baked at the highest temperature possible without burning the crust. For a good bake, the internal crumb temperature must reach 203-205°F (95 to 96°C). For a one pound loaf of white pan bread baked in a gas reel oven, this should be accomplished in about 16 minutes at 450°F (232°C). Hamburger buns should be baked in nine to ten minutes at 435°F (224°C). Lower baking temperatures and longer baking times will increase the *bake-out loss* for the bread

Experimental bread loaves baked in 1600 cc pans cooling on wire screen.

and rolls to more than 10% of the dough scaling weight. Deck and electric ovens tend to require more time for baking the same product. Sometimes the controls in these types of ovens, especially in older models, are in locations which do not reflect the true baking temperature because the sensors are shielded from the heat source and the response of the controls to temperature changes is delayed.

Depanning and Cooling

The baked bread and rolls should be removed from the baking pans as quickly as possible. The product should then be allowed to cool under ambient conditions and without significant air movement over them. To prevent "sweating" of the loaves and rolls, they should be placed on wire racks which allow air movement all around the product. While bread takes about one hour to cool to ambient temperature, buns may require only 30 minutes.

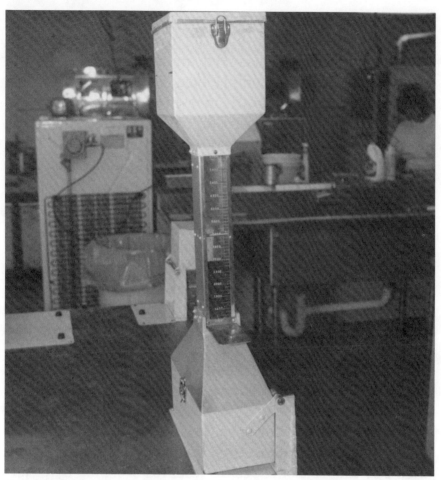

A volumeter makes determining product volume much easier for the experimental baker.

Determination of Product Volume

After cooling, all test product should be weighed and measured for volume by rapeseed displacement (*Loaf Volumeter* available from TMCO, National Manufacturing in Lincoln, NE). Rapeseeds are ideal for this purpose, because they are light and round, so that they flow well around the product to be measured and they tend to fill all voids in the measuring container. A volumeter with a calibration block saves much time in measuring product volumes.

A more complex and time consuming method utilizes a sturdy container filled level to the top with clean rapeseed. After removing the measured amount of rapeseed, the bread is placed in the empty box. The container is then refilled with a portion of the measured rapeseed. The volume of the displaced rapeseed, i.e., seed no longer fitting into the measuring container, is determined with a large graduated cylinder and is equal to the volume of the measured baked product.

Specific Volume

The volume of loaves and rolls is usually reported either in terms of total cubic centimeters (cc), or as specific volume. The specific volume is expressed as cubic centimeters per gram (cc/g) of bread or rolls. This value is obtained by dividing the volume of the loaf or rolls by the weight of the unit(s) in grams. To convert cc/g to cubic inch per ounce (cub inch/oz), multiply the cc/g value by 1.73.

Since the weight of baked foods is directly affected by the baking process, too much or too little bake can have a significant effect on the specific volume. Overbaked product is lighter and yields an erroneously high specific volume. For this reason, specific volumes obtained by different baking laboratories should never be compared with one another. Specific volume data should also never be considered as absolute values. The real value of specific volume data is limited to a comparison of product prepared in the same baking laboratory under identical controlled conditions.

Average specific volume data for properly baked white pan bread range from about 5.4 cc/g for product made from a medium quality winter wheat flour, to 6.2 cc/g for equivalent product prepared from a very good quality spring wheat flour.

Control of Loaf Volume

When a flour is test-baked, the technologist studies its bread-making potential. It does not mean that a larger specific volume is always desirable. In the commercial manufacture of pan bread, too much loaf volume is as detrimental as too little. What is most important in bread production is **consistency**. The loaf volume should not vary significantly from day to day. Small loaves will not fill the bread bags properly, and larger loaves will not fit into the bags without major difficulties during the bagging operation.

Fortunately, experienced bakers know how to control bread volume with minor changes in proof time and, if necessary, by varying the amount of yeast in the formula. The *oven kick* (expansion of loaves during baking) depends on three conditions: extensibility of the dough, gas retention of the dough, and gas production during the early baking phase, i.e., the amount of yeast activity. The more yeast is available in the dough, the more gas will be produced as the dough temperature increases during baking and before the yeast is killed by the heat. If this gas is retained by the dough and the dough does not resist expansion, then the loaves will have a good oven expansion or, as the baker calls it, "oven kick." This, of course, assumes there is sufficient fermentable sugar available for the yeast to utilize.

Packaging

The test product is usually packaged for evaluation on the following day. For shelf-life evaluation, yeast-raised bakery foods should be packaged in two individually tied polyethylene bread or bun bags and stored for the appropriate length of time at 77°F (25°C) in an environmental cabinet or in a protected area. Firming of bread crumb is very much influenced by changes in the ambient tempera-

ture during storage. Cooler storage temperatures accelerate the process of *starch retrogradation* (crumb firming or
staling).

Product Evaluation

Except for the volume, which is based on objective measurements, all other quality values are based on subjec-
tive judgments and personal opinions. There is also a vast
difference in the philosophy of *scoring* experimental bread
versus commercial product. Scoring is expressing specific
product quality characteristics, such as crust color and
crumb texture, in numerical values.

Commercially produced bread is not "scored" for the
effect of a specific ingredient on product quality, but how
well the employees controlled the manufacture of bread
relative to specifications set by management. This takes
into account not only the general quality of the bread, but
also its weight, slicing, and the packaging. Although the
flavor of bread is very important to the consumer, this quality characteristic seldom receives much attention from production personnel, since it is assumed that the taste is constant from day to day. Significant adjustments in the product formulation to improve the flavor profile may also require changes in labeling and are, therefore, no longer a
viable option. All major effort is, therefore, directed towards
manufacturing baked foods with a good eye appeal. This
includes proper packaging and a uniform crumb grain.

Experimental baking is done for a different purpose. It
is done to study the effect of a specific variable (ingredient
or processing) on various product quality characteristics.
This also includes dough handling properties. Stiff or soft
and sticky doughs indicate an imperfect formula balance
and the potential for problems in a bakery during large-
scale dough processing. The product quality itself is deter-

mined by three different sets of characteristics:
- Appearance (including loaf volume)
- Crumb structure and color
- Eating (sensory) quality.

The following table lists these characteristics and defines the desired traits for white pan bread. Most of these quality attributes also apply to hamburger buns (Appendix B provides a sample score sheet and Appendix C provides a list of descriptors for bread evaluation).

Quality Characteristics

External: (30 points)	
Volume:	Large and without significant shrinkage.
Symmetry:	Uniform expansion. Rounded top. No bulging.
Crust Color:	Uniform golden brown. No blotches.
Break & Shred:	Uniform and straight break. Smooth and even shred.

Note: Crust should be smooth and without blisters.

Crumb Structure: (35 points)	
Texture:	Soft and "silky." Moist, but not tacky. Resilient crumb structure.
Grain:	Uniform cell structure. Cells elongated. Thin cell walls.
Crumb Color:	White with a "creamy" (faint yellow) hue.

Sensory: (35 points)	
Aroma:	Light fermentation aroma. No "off" (foreign) or "sour" odors.

Taste:	Must be pleasant. No sour or "off-taste."
Mouthfeel:	When chewed, product should neither be crumbly, nor gummy or tough. Crumb should not give a dry or wet mouthfeel, but must masticate well.

When the baking technologist scores the test bread, care must be taken to not penalize the test variable for improper processing procedures and for poor equipment adjustment, e.g. wrong moulder settings, and poor slicing (dull blades or knife).

Since the appearance and crumb structure of bread can be affected as much by dough processing as by formulation, it is of utmost importance that every test-baking of ingredients is done under strictly controlled conditions. Also, it is very unlikely that a baking laboratory can reproduce all processing conditions of a large commercial bakery. Therefore, bread prepared in a small baking laboratory will almost always look different from commercially produced bread. Just as it is important to control all the processing parameters when ingredients are tested for their functionality, it is equally important to control the quality of the ingredients when processing parameters are evaluated.

Since bread *stales* and develops a firm and dry crumb structure more rapidly at cooler temperatures, it is very important that loaves stored for shelf-life evaluation are kept at a constant temperature and are prevented from drying out. Although much of the European research is done at 68°F (20°C), in the United States people prefer the slightly more comfortable "room temperature" of 75 or 77°F (24 or 25°C). These temperatures are more representative for those found in most American homes and the results are, therefore, more valid for this country than those obtained at the cooler European temperature. But regardless of what temperature is chosen for this type of study, all product in a test series must be stored under the same conditions.

It is recommended to keep the test product in random order. An environmental cabinet with an independently controlled heating and cooling capacity is preferred for storing product for a shelf-life test. It is also best when the individual loaves are packaged in two polyethylene bread bags instead of in only one, and each bag is closed and tied individually with a twist tie. This will reduce the loss of moisture during storage to almost zero. Since this type of packaging does not allow any moisture to escape, there is no need to worry about the relative humidity in the environmental cabinet. The relative humidity in the atmosphere surrounding the bakery food in a closed container, in this case tied bread bags, will always be in equilibrium with the product's water activity and is independent of the ambient moisture conditions in the cabinet.

There are two different methods for measuring the progress of the crumb staling process. While one method measures changes in crumb softness, the other measures changes in crumb firmness. If the obtained values become smaller with decreasing softness of the crumb, we measure *crumb softness*. If, however, the values grow larger with aging of the product, then *crumb firmness* is measured.

Methods for measuring crumb softness utilize a constant force (weight of compression plunger) acting on a specified area of the bread crumb for a given period of time. The penetration of the compression plunger into the bread crumb during this time period is measured in tenths of millimeters. The distance of penetration (deformation) decreases as the bread loses its softness with time. Thus, **crumb softness is measured as the amount of deformation produced by a constant force**. The *Penetrometer* is a typical representative of instruments measuring crumb softness.

Crumb firmness is the measured amount of force required to produce a constant deformation in the bread crumb. This is accomplished by measuring the force needed to compress (deform) a specified area of the bread crumb with a plunger by a predetermined distance or by a percentage of the product's thickness. One such procedure is described by Method 74-09 published by the American Association of Cereal Chemists (AACC). This method recommends compressing two slices of bread (one inch total thickness) with a 36 millimeter diameter flat disk by 6.2 millimeter (25% of one inch) at the rate of 100 millimeter compression per minute. The Instron Corporation, Stevens Advanced Weighing Systems, and Texture Technologies Corporation are offering suitable instrumentation for this type of evaluation. Most of the models available from these manufacturers can now be interfaced to computers. But as always, the more sophisticated and flexible the instrument is, the greater its cost. However, there is also a simple instrument available which was designed specifically for testing bakery foods. The *Baker Compressimeter* can be used to measure either the softness or the firmness of bread, and it is available from the F. Watkins Corporation. The AACC has published an official method (74-10) for using this relatively inexpensive instrument.

Primary Ingredients

Of the four primary ingredients used for bread and roll production, flour and yeast have probably the greatest effect on the final product quality. The wrong flour or a poor quality yeast will have an adverse effect on product quality. A proper amount of clean and potable water is necessary to form a pliable dough. But only in rare cases does water quality affect dough handling and crumb structure. Salt (sodium chloride) is a relatively pure chemical. It contributes not only taste, but it has also functional properties in doughs and in the crumb structure of baked product.

Flour

The type of flour used by the baker can vary not only according to its source: wheat, rye, barley, corn (maize), oats, amaranth, millet, etc., but also with respect to its grind or physical shape: fine or medium grind flour, cracked or flaked grains, and in the way it is refined or separated from unwanted components of the grain: patent flour, straight grade flour, whole meal. The type of grain product used in the manufacture of bread will not only affect the taste and texture of the baked product, but also the technology used and the final shape and size of the food. The reason why corn masa is baked in the shape of a tortilla, rather than in a loaf, is the total absence of a structure forming protein in corn. This structure forming protein found only in wheat is called *wheat gluten*. Proteins present in other grains are often called *gluten*, too, but these proteins do not form a three-dimensional cell structure, like wheat gluten does. Corn gluten, a by-product in the manufacture of corn starch and corn syrup, is not suitable for bread dough formation and is generally used as an animal feed.

Flour Quality

In the United States and Canada, the most suitable and commonly used flour for the manufacture of bread or bread-like bakery foods is milled from hard wheat grown in the region located between the Missouri River in the east and the Rocky Mountains in the West, and in the Canadian provinces north of this area. The dry climate in this region is ideal for the formation of the two wheat flour protein components which make up gluten when the flour milled from this wheat is blended with water and subjected to mechanical energy (mixing). Generally, the wheat grown in the southern states of this hard wheat region has a lower protein content than the wheat cultivated in the northern states. Winter wheat grown in northwest Texas, Oklahoma, Kansas, eastern Colorado, southern Nebraska and South Dakota is planted in the fall and is harvested in late spring or early summer. Spring wheat, grown in eastern Montana, North Dakota, and western Minnesota is sown in the spring and harvested in late summer or early fall. While some of the white wheat grown in Washington, Oregon, and Idaho is milled for local consumption, much of it is exported.

Until the advent of continuous bread dough mixing, flour milled from spring wheat, which is also known as "northwest wheat flour" with a protein content of normally 12% or more, was clearly preferred over the "southwestern wheat flour" milled from winter wheat and having a protein content of usually less than 12%. Over the years, however, the protein content of a typical bread flour used by the wholesale baking industry dropped from 12.5-12.75% in the 1950s, to 11.75-12.25% twenty years later, and to the even lower level of 10.8-11.5% frequently found in bread flours today. Flours with a higher protein level are still used today, but only by small retail bakers or for the production of specialty bread products.

As the protein level of the bread flour decreased over time, the amount of ash in the flour increased dramatically from about 0.42-0.44% in the 1970s to 0.48-0.52% twenty years later. The ash content reflects the amount of flour the miller "extracts" from 100 lbs. of wheat. In normal growing years, a miller is now able to get a yield of about 74 lbs. of flour from every 100 lbs. of wheat grist (grain mix prepared for grinding or milling), instead of the 72 to 73 lbs. of flour the miller extracted from the same amount of wheat 20 years ago. With new milling techniques, the miller is now able to separate the wheat germ and the bran from the wheat kernel with less loss of the adjacent endosperm, or starchy interior of the wheat kernel. Since the ash and protein contents of the endosperm increase from the center of the kernel to the outside, and the gluten quality of the protein tends to decrease in the same direction, a flour with the same protein content but a higher ash content may not be of as good a baking quality as a similar flour with a lower ash content.

Selection of Flour

The functionality of wheat flour in the formulation is of utmost importance. The quality of the finished product depends on how the wheat protein is developed into a three-dimensional gluten matrix, whose function is to entrap carbon dioxide during fermentation and to form the cell structure supporting the product. This cell structure affects the bread volume, texture and shelf-life.

In general, the miller and flour broker can best recommend which type and brand of flour is most suitable for a given application. The availability of a wide range of wheat flour in this country and the competition between mills favor the baking industry. Any bakery buying truckload quantities, in bags or in bulk, can choose the flour it deems best for its products. The only limiting factor will be cost, including the cost of transportation. However, the baker must always keep in mind that the "cheapest" ingredient is seldom the most economical ingredient! Losses incurred through the production of inferior or unsatisfactory bakery foods, or the use of expensive additives to correct deficiencies of "cheap" ingredients, can easily outweigh the gains obtained by buying a low-cost, but inferior flour.

Specifications for Bread Flour

Most ingredient specifications used by bakeries are written by the ingredient suppliers and not by the baker. Therefore, ingredient specifications are merely a description of what the vendor or miller is able to supply to meet the baker's needs. Generally, samples fitting the description in the specification had previously been test-baked under normal manufacturing conditions and were found to function as desired by the baker. The physical and compositional description of the test-sample then became, almost automatically, its "specification" by simply replacing single numbers with ranges or limiting values. In most cases, this method is adequate. Other competing suppliers will often provide similar, but still different sets of specifications for ingredients to be used interchangeably with the first product. Because mills often buy the wheat they mill in different growing areas, it is not always easy for them to match flour functionality exactly with all the specification values of another mill, unless the baker is willing to pay a premium price. Therefore, specifications for ingredients may vary slightly from supplier to supplier and, sometimes, also from crop year to crop year.

Each ingredient specification consists of two major sections:

a. Section written by the vendor (manufacturer or broker), and
b. Section written by the user (bakery).

In the case of flour, the vendor will usually supply the information in the following areas:

    1. Analytical:
        Moisture content range or maximum value
        Protein content range
        Ash content range
        Alpha-amylase activity range
        Starch damage (if requested)
        Particle size (if requested)
    2. Rheological:
        Absorption (% of water absorbed by flour)
        Mixing requirement
        Tolerance of flour to mixing
    3. Microbiological:
        Total count of microbes per gram of flour
        Count of mold spores
        Count of wild yeast cells

The bakery generally will, or should, specify the following conditions:

1. **Flour must produce consistent results from shipment to shipment and must perform like approved initial production sample!**
2. Flour must/must not be enriched with vitamins and minerals to specified standard levels.
3. Flour must be milled, stored, and delivered to the bakery under sanitary conditions.

4. No extraneous matter in the flour beyond limits set by government regulations.
5. Flour must be delivered to the bakery as scheduled and specified (in bulk or bags).

There may be additional instructions in the specifications, such as flour treatment, the type of wheat used for the flour, and specific performance test requirements. When the bakery takes delivery of an entire truckload at a time, the bakery may request copies of analytical and test data for that particular flour shipment. Also, every specification value should be given with the respective testing method with which these results are obtained. A sample of a typical specification sheet for regular bread flour is shown in Table I.

The average baker should really not be too interested in the numbers or values stated in the specification, nor should these values be used as a legal basis for confrontations with the supplier. The only interest the baker should have is that the flour, or any other ingredient, conforms with government regulations for potential adulteration and that it functions properly in formulations and without drastic changes in the production technology used. Also, the flour or ingredient must not, in any way, present a health hazard to employees or customers. An ingredient specification should also not give the supplier a license to ship to the baker an inferior product which still meets most or all specifications. A typical example for such a product would be a flour contaminated with heat-stable microorganisms which produce an off-color and/or a foreign aroma in the bread crumb. The federal government has established guidelines for maximum allowable levels of toxins in flour from pesticides and mold (aflatoxin and vomitoxin). These guidelines are generally more of a concern to the miller than to the baker.

Table I
Ingredient Specification

Premium Bread Company, Inc.   Preparer: Jane B. Baker
Ingredient: Pan Bread Flour   Ingredient Code: 101120
Date Issued: August 27, 1993
Date Approved: September 8, 1993 By: Joe M. Overhead
Last Revision:

Ingredient Description: Bakery flour milled from sound hard red winter wheat or from a blend of such wheat and hard red spring wheat.
Appearance: Flour must have a clean and white appearance.
Odor and Taste: No unusual off-odor or off-taste.
Packaging: Bulk shipment in tanker truck or railcar.

Analytical Values:	Standard			Test Method
Moisture %	13.5	±	0.5	AACC 44-15A
Protein (14% M.B.*) %	11.5	±	0.5	AACC 46-12
Ash (14% M.B.) %	0.49	±	0.02	AACC 08-01
Starch Damage %	7.0	±	2.0	AACC 76-30A

* 14% Moisture Basis (calculated for a 14% moisture content)

Rheological Performance:				
Dough Water Absorption %	59.5	±	2.0	AACC 54-21
Arrival Time, minutes	2.0	±	0.5	AACC 54-21
Peak Time, minutes	7.5	±	1.5	AACC 54-21
Departure Time, minutes	15.0	±	2.0	AACC 54-21
Stability Time, minutes	13.0	±	2.5	AACC 54-21
Mixing Tolerance Index, BU	30.0	±	10.0	AACC 54-21

Alpha Amylase Activity:				
Amylograph Viscosity, BU	500.0	±	50.0	AACC 22-10
or Falling Number, seconds	220.0	±	20.0	AACC 56-81B

Flour Treatment:
All flour is to be bleached with benzoyl peroxide and treated with 10 parts per million azodicarbonamide to enhance its performance.

Extraneous Matter:	None	AACC

Microbial Contamination:		
Total Count	< 50,000/gram	BAM
Salmonella	Negative	BAM
E. Coli	< 10/gram	BAM
Yeast	<250/gram	BAM
Mold	<1000/gram	BAM

Enrichment:	Nutrient:	mg/100g Flour
	Thiamin (Vitamin B1)	0.64
	Riboflavin (Vitamin B2)	0.40
	Niacin (Vitamin B3)	5.30
	Iron, Reduced	4.40
	Calcium	212

Performance Testing of Flour

There are two philosophies regarding testing flour for performance. Users of large quantities of flour generally insist on testing a sample from every shipment of flour for its performance in white pan bread. A technician usually evaluates the dough rheology of the flour with one of the following instruments:

- Farinograph (Brabender)
- Alveograph (Chopin)
- Mixograph (TMCO National Mfg. Co.)
- Rheograph (Interstate Brands Corp.)

Standardized flour testing procedures have been developed for all instruments except the Rheograph. All instruments give reproducible results, which are generally recorded continuously as graphs. While the Alveograph measures the ability of a dough piece to stretch into a bubble under controlled conditions, the graphs produced by the other three instruments reflect changes in the torque exerted by the dough's viscosity on the shaft of the mixing attachment.

Since the configuration of the mixing bowl and the mixing attachment is different in each instrument, the graphs produced by them differ significantly. Farinograms and alveograms are relatively easy to interpret, but it takes some experience to properly evaluate the mixograms and the rheograms. Each of these four instruments has its advocates and critics and they will all indicate any significant changes in the flour quality and in the amount of water needed to form an extensible dough.

Farinograph

The Brabender Farinograph is the most popular dough rheology instrument used for measuring dough-making properties of flour because the farinograms are relatively easy to interpret. Newer models of this instrument can also be interfaced with computers. Although none of the data can be applied directly to the manufacture of bread, they do provide valuable guidelines for formulating and mixing doughs. The dough water *absorption* indicates how much water must be added to the flour in order to obtain a dough of a desirable viscosity. For bread flour, the viscosity curve is usually centered on the 500 BU line at its peak. The *arrival time* indicates how quickly the flour hydrates (pick-up time). The *peak time* tells us how fast the dough "develops," i.e., the gluten develops. The *dough stability* time indicates the tolerance of the dough to mixing, while the *Mixing Tolerance Index* (MTI) indicates how fast the dough breaks down when it is overmixed.

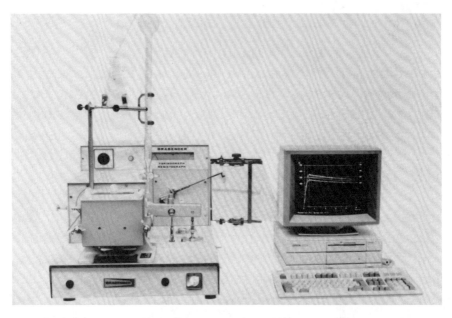

A Farinograph. (Photo courtesy of C.W. Brabender Instruments, Inc.).

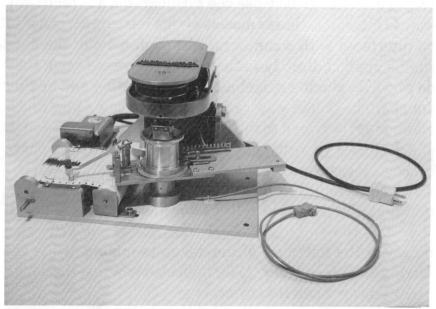

A Mixograph. (Photo courtesy of National Manufacturing, TMCO).

Mixograph

The Mixograph is a small pin mixer for doughs with a recording device or a computer attached to it. However, it requires more experience for the proper interpretation of the parameters. The proper absorption (dough viscosity) is interpreted from the width and regularity of the recorded graph. The *peak time* is related to the time needed to develop the gluten structure in the dough, and the height of the peak is one of the indicators for the bread-making quality of the wheat protein in the flour sample. Lines drawn through the middle of the curves before and after the peak and intersecting at the peak, form the *dough strengthening angle*, which gives an indication of flour strength. The angle between the line drawn through the intersect and parallel to the baseline and the line drawn through the middle of the curve after the peak, is called the *dough weak-*

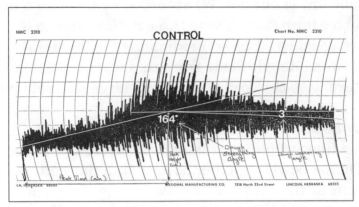

An indication of flour strength is provided by the dough strengthening angle and dough weakening angle on the Mixogram.

A Mixogram.

ening angle. A relatively large dough weakening angle shown by a steep descent of the curve after the peak implies that the dough lacks tolerance to overmixing. A good strong bread flour has relatively wide bands in the mixogram and the curve shows only a mild downward slope after it has reached its peak.

Alveograph

The Alveograph is widely used in Europe and is based on a different principle. Whereas the Farinograph and the Mixograph measure changes in dough viscosity during extended mixing, the Alveograph mixes the dough with a standard absorption (76% of total flour solids with flour moisture as part of the standard 76% absorption) and for a standard time. The developed dough is then extruded, sheeted and cut into patties which, after a predetermined amount of rest time, are subjected to air pressure which blows the dough patty into a bubble until it bursts. The instrument records the initial resistance of the dough to expansion (P), the extensibility of the dough (L), and the total amount of energy (W) absorbed by the dough during the bubble formation. These three indicators and the ratio P/L are considered to be predictions for the ability of an actual bread dough made from this flour to form a grain structure with thin cell walls and a large loaf volume.

Rheograph

The Rheograph is actually a Hobart A-200 mixer with a McDuffee bowl (a mixing bowl with a flat bottom and a fixed pin in the center and a two-prong dough developer orbiting around the center pin in the bowl). The mixer is situated in an air conditioned cabinet and the torque on the mixing shaft is recorded as a vertical straight curve which gradually becomes narrower. The end point of this test is the total breakdown of the dough structure, or the *fatigue time*, measured in minutes.

Flour Additives

Additives are added to flour for three different reasons: vitamin and mineral enrichment; improvement of flour performance and improvement of flour appearance.

While the first two types of additives can also be added directly to doughs at the bakery, the bleaching process for the flour takes time and must be accomplished before the flour is used as an ingredient.

Flour Enrichment

The need to enrich bakery products with vitamins (thiamin, niacin, and riboflavin) is no longer as important as it was when the enrichment program was initiated to eliminate the deficiency of these three vitamins in the American diet before and during World War II. Many nutritional experts agree today that enriching flour and bread with these B-vitamins is no longer necessary, while others advocate the inclusion of folic acid in this program. Listing thiamin, niacin, and riboflavin is no longer required by the Food and Drug Administration in the new Nutrition Labeling and Education Act of 1990 (NLEA), unless enrichment with vitamins is part of a nutritional claim.

The Code of Federal Regulations for *enriched bread and rolls* (21 CFR Ch. I Part 136.115) requires that "...each such food contains in each pound 1.8 milligrams of thiamin, 1.1 milligrams of riboflavin, 15 milligrams of niacin, and 12.5 milligrams of iron." The requirements for *enriched flour* are that "...it contains in each pound 2.9 milligrams of thiamin, 1.8 milligrams of riboflavin, 24 milligrams of niacin, and 20 milligrams of iron."

While calcium is an optional enrichment ingredient, the NLEA requires that the amount of calcium in a serving of food be declared as *% Daily Reference Value* (DRV). The DRV is based on the recommended daily intake of the nutrient component for an adult, which is one gram or 1000 milligrams (mg) of calcium per adult.

The quantity of iron added to wheat flour as enrichment is based on the amount of this element lost when wheat is milled into white flour. Iron may be added either as *reduced iron* (electrolytic iron or iron reduced with hydrogen), or as a salt of inorganic or organic acids, such as ferrous sulfate, ferric orthophosphate, and ferrous fumarate. Iron, too, must be listed on the new label as % DRV, which has been established as 18 milligrams (mg) per adult.

Flour Improvers

Since much of the flour used by bread bakers is now shipped in bulk and used within a few days after milling, the flour no longer has the time to "age" at the mill or in the bakery. The aging of flour was once considered to be essential for its proper performance. During aging, flour absorbs oxygen from the air. This results in a beneficial modification of the protein in the flour. Old time bakers took advantage of this phenomenon and stored their flour in woven cotton bags for three to four weeks in a room with good air circulation. Some of them even restacked the flour bags periodically, so that the bags came into contact with fresh air. The bakers also noted that three or four days after the flour was milled, there was a period of five to seven days when the flour produced sticky doughs and small loaves. They referred to this period as the *sweating period* and the unaged flour was called *green flour*.

Maturing Agents

As bakeries grew larger and their daily usage of very large quantities of flour made the storage and handling of flour in bags impractical, millers started to add chemical oxidizing agents to the flour to eliminate the long storage time during which the flour was allowed to *age* naturally. Although chlorine dioxide and nitrogen trichloride were widely used to age flour during the early years of flour treatment, these chemicals are no longer extensively used in the United States and they have been replaced primarily with 5-10 ppm azodicarbonamide (ADA) added to white flour milled from hard red winter wheat, or with 10-20 ppm potassium bromate in white flour milled from hard red spring wheat. Bakers and millers are now encouraged by the Food and Drug Administration (FDA) to discontinue the use of potassium bromate for the manufacture of bakery foods and many millers have started to substitute 20-40 ppm ascorbic acid (AA) or blends of ascorbic acid and ADA for potassium bromate. Iodates and other potential flour oxidants, too, have been investigated for this purpose.

While the addition of potassium bromate to flour must be declared as such in the ingredient statement, azodicarbonamide is legally declared as a *bleaching agent*, even though it has no whitening effect on flour.

While Canada limits the amount of ascorbic acid in flour to 200 ppm, there is currently no restriction on its addition to flours milled in the United States. Even though ascorbic acid is also known as Vitamin C, the baker cannot claim the addition of this vitamin, since Vitamin C loses its vitamin function during dough processing and baking. In fact, the baker does not need to declare any addition of this dough improver, since it is considered to be merely a processing aid and not a component of the finished product.

Enzymes in Flour

Millers are generally requested to standardize the alpha-amylase activity in flours used for the production of yeast-raised (yeast-leavened) bakery foods. The natural alpha-amylase activity in wheat flour varies with the climatic conditions which existed when the wheat was harvested. When the weather is very warm and dry at harvest time, the wheat and the flour milled from it will have a very low alpha-amylase activity. Conversely, when wet weather delays the harvest of mature wheat, the sprouting process begins in some of the kernels, especially in those which have absorbed moisture, and are prevented from drying rapidly after the rain has stopped.

Sprouting, or germination, depends on the formation and activation of many enzymes in the seed. Alpha amylase is one of these enzymes which helps convert the starch in the wheat kernel to sugar and energy needed for the germ to grow into a plant. Even though sprouting is a desirable trait in a seed, the presence of an excessive amount of enzymes formed during this process detracts from the baking quality of the flour milled from *sprout damaged* wheat. However, some alpha-amylase activity in the flour is desirable, since it provides fermentable sugars for the yeast, particularly in flour preferments such as liquid and plastic sponges.

Unless the baker prefers an untreated flour, the miller generally standardizes the flour with diastatic (containing amylase enzymes) barley malt to an alpha-amylase activity of 450-550 Brabender Units (BU), when measuring this activity with a Brabender Viscograph (Amylograph), or to a range of 225 to 275 seconds with the Falling Number instrument.

Both instruments measure the viscosity of a standard starch or flour paste heated at a controlled rate. The Falling Number instrument does this much more quickly than the older Amylograph. The values obtained with either instrument vary inversely with the alpha-amylase activity, i.e., a higher value in BU (Amylograph) or in seconds (Falling Number) will indicate a lower amylolitic activity. This is because the value produced by either instrument reflects the viscosity of the flour-water paste, which decreases as the alpha amylase breaks down the starch paste.

Although the American milling and baking industries still prefer to use barley malt for standardizing the alpha-amylase activity in bread flours, millers in most other countries prefer the use of similar enzymes from a fungal source. The thermal death point (temperature, at which the enzymes are inactivated) of fungal amylase is about 10-15°F (5-8°C) lower than for cereal (malt) amylase. This difference in the sensitivity of the enzymes to elevated temperatures also makes it impossible to measure the activity of fungal alpha-amylase with the standard methods developed for measuring the activity of enzymes found in barley malt. Modified methods are now available for measuring the enzymatic activity of fungal enzymes in flour, but the optimum values are quite different from those recommended for flour treated with cereal amylase.

Flour Bleaching

Bakers like to produce white breads with a very light crumb color, even though they no longer make claims to that effect. Wheat contains naturally yellow pigments in the endosperm, the starchy interior of the wheat kernel. These pigments tend to impart a yellowish tint to the flour milled from it. The types of pigments (xanthophyll, carotene, flavones, etc.) and the amounts present vary with the wheat variety. When the baker specifies a bleached flour, the miller will treat the flour with a *bleaching agent* to destroy the pigments. The bleaching process takes place by oxidation of "unsaturated carbon chains" (containing a double bond between two adjacent carbon atoms) in the coloring bodies.

The most effective and widely used bleaching agent for bread flours is *benzoyl peroxide*. Its action is not instantaneous and it requires several days before the bleaching action is complete. The "normal" application rate for this treatment agent, a solid, is about 50 ppm; but it may vary from 30-100 ppm, depending on the wheat variety. Benzoyl peroxide has no maturing effect on the flour and it is, therefore, often used in combination with ADA, which has no bleaching effect. However, whether the flour is treated with one or with both of these oxidizing agents, it must be labeled as "bleached."

Another bleaching agent is *chlorine dioxide*. This flour treatment agent is really a better maturing agent than it is a bleaching compound for flour pigments. Chlorine dioxide has been used since 1948, primarily for all-purpose flours. It is added to the flour at a rate of about 15 ppm.

Wheat Flour Types

Besides the regular bread flour described previously in this chapter, there are other wheat flour types available to the baker. With the advent of roller mills, the miller is able to separate the products of different milling steps into separate *streams* which he can recombine to flours of different baking qualities.

Milling of Flour

The overall flour quality is determined by two major phases of milling:

1. Extraction of flour from the wheat.
2. Separation and recombination of flour streams.

Flour Extraction

White flour is produced by *extracting* as much of the starchy part of the grain kernel as possible by removing the bran coat and the germ from the *stock* (broken up grain). The *extraction rate* of flour (pounds of flour recovered from 100 lbs. wheat) is dependent on several factors:

1. Milling quality of the wheat.
2. Milling technology used.
3. Relative cost of flour and mill feed.
4. Moisture content of wheat.

For many years, the extraction rate for wheat averaged about 72%. However, since the late 1970s, millers started to gradually increase this rate until they now recover up to 76 lbs. of flour from 100 lbs. of wheat. The remainder consists of bran, wheat germ, and *shorts* (a mixture of bran, germ, and flour). Although some of the bran and wheat germ is recovered for human consumption, most of it is sold with the shorts as animal feed.

The price for mill feed has a significant effect on the cost of flour and, to a lesser extent, also on flour quality. If the price for mill feed is relatively high, then the miller can sell the flour at a slightly lower price. Conversely, when the miller receives very little for the mill feed fractions, more must be charged for the flour to offset his milling cost. This market condition will also induce the miller to extract more flour from the grist and to produce less mill feed.

Flour Separation

With the advent of roller mills, the miller is able to separate the extracted flour into different *streams* or fractions of flour produced by the various milling steps, which are selectively recombined to obtain flour of a specified quality.

Millers can *separate* their flours into two groups: *patent flour* and *clear flour*. Patent flour comes from the innermost parts of the endosperm in the wheat kernel. Clear flour comes from the outer portion of the endosperm. Depending on how much clear flour the miller withholds from the patent flour, the miller can produce a variety of patent and clear flours. By combining all the extracted flour streams, the miller obtains a *straight grade flour*. By removing the "worst" 5% portion, or the *second clear flour*, from the flour, the miller produces a *long patent flour*. Most of the flour sold now to large bread bakeries is either a straight grade or a long patent flour milled from hard wheat. The second clear flour is of low baking quality with relatively high ash and protein levels, and it is "separated" from all grades of patent flour.

The approximate separation ratios for extracted flour are as follows:

40 to 60% Fancy Patent + 35 to 55% Fancy Clear Flour
60 to 70% First Patent + 25 to 35% Fancy Clear Flour
70 to 80% Short Patent + 15 to 25% Clear Flour
80 to 90% Medium Patent + 5 to 15% Clear Flour
90 to 95% Long Patent + 0 to 5% Clear Flour

As the separation of patent flour increases from 40-95% of the extracted flour, the ash and the protein contents in the flour increase, too; but the overall quality of the flour tends to decrease slightly. The fancy patent and first patent flours and the corresponding fancy clear flour are not available from hard wheat flour and thus have no significance for the manufacture of bread products.

While the straight and patent flours are used for white and specialty breads and for sweet and puff pastries, the clear flour finds applications in dark and mixed grain breads. Since very few large bakeries still use the better grades of patent flour, clear flour is no longer inexpensive and readily available. Therefore, many bakers now use their regular bread flour with some vital wheat gluten added in place of clear flour.

Whole Wheat Products

There are various types of whole wheat products available to the baker. They differ primarily in their physical shape and how they are manufactured. Since whole wheat contains the wheat germ with higher levels of fat and enzymes, it does not keep as well as white flour. Its shelf-life is limited to a few months, even under ideal conditions. Whole wheat products cannot only become rancid, but their bran portion also acquires a bitter taste which becomes stronger with time.

Whole wheat is available in three different grinds (fine, medium, and coarse), flaked, steel cut, cracked, crushed and stone ground. Because the protein in the coarser varieties of whole wheat is only partially available for gluten formation and most of the protein in the bran portion is incapable of forming gluten, most of the whole wheat products are manufactured from spring wheat with a higher protein level, which can range from 12% to as high as 15% or higher.

Whole Wheat Bread must be, by law, made from only whole wheat products. It cannot contain any white flour. The Standard of Identity for Whole Wheat Bread neither permits, nor prohibits, the use of vital wheat gluten. The use of vital wheat gluten, therefore, falls under the law for *Good Manufacturing Practices* which states that no ingredient or additive shall be used at amounts greater than necessary to achieve the desired effects.

In contrast to whole wheat bread, regular *Wheat Bread* has no standard of identity and may be manufactured with varying amounts of whole wheat products and white flour. The whole wheat products in these types of bread generally range from a low of 20% to a high of 70% of the total flour. Again, the use of vital wheat gluten in wheat breads is governed by Good Manufacturing Practices.

Water

Although water is a major ingredient in bakery foods, there is not total agreement on how much "water quality" affects "product quality." This discussion goes back to the early part of this century, when a major baking company wanted to standardize the quality of its bread produced in a number of different locations. When this attempt failed, even though all the bakeries were using ingredients from the same suppliers, it was concluded that the observed differences were due to "inconsistencies in water quality." The chemical analysis of water samples from these bakeries verified that there were significant differences in water hardness, impurities, and pH of the various samples. This finding led to the development of the first *mineral yeast food* by Fleischmann. This dough additive contained the buffering salt calcium sulfate to minimize differences in water hardness and acidity (pH). The salts ammonium sulfate or ammonium chloride were included in this compounded ingredient to stimulate propagation of yeast cells in fermenting sponges and dough, thus contributing to the descriptive name "yeast food."

Although the use of mineral yeast food in bread doughs helped to overcome differences in "water quality," the effect of water on product quality has never been fully answered. In fact, it is suspected that the topic of water quality is often used as "the last excuse" for the inability of bakery production management to solve quality problems in their product. Only in communities with a supply of very soft water or with water having a high degree of alkalinity or acidity may bakeries have to resort to more drastic measures than to merely add mineral yeast food (MYF) to their doughs. The manufacturers of bakery ingredients now offer *acid type yeast foods* (containing monocalcium phosphate) for bakers who must use alkaline water, and calcium carbonate to buffer very acidic conditions in bread dough.

Yeast

Yeast is a living microorganism and is susceptible to injury and even death when subjected to adverse conditions during storage and handling. While the baker uses what is known as baker's yeast (*Saccharomyces cerevisiae*) to leaven products, the brewer of beer uses *brewer's yeast* and the wine maker uses other specific yeasts. Not all of these yeasts are suitable for leavening doughs. There are also "wild" yeasts (i.e., yeasts occurring naturally in the environment) everywhere. While some of these wild yeasts may cause food spoilage, others may be useful. Bakers preparing their own spontaneous sours depend on the desirable wild yeast strains. The microbial culture used for the manufacture of the authentic San Francisco Sour Bread contains a very specific yeast (*Saccharomyces exiguus*) which is, unlike baker's yeast, unable to ferment maltose. However, this yeast is able to coexist with the heterofermentative *Lactobacillus sanfrancisco* which produces several different organic acids besides lactic acid at pH levels as low as 3.8 to 4.5. This special yeast for sour doughs is an excellent producer of the leavening gas carbon dioxide, but it does not tolerate freezing as well as the *lactobacillus* organism and some other yeast varieties.

Baker's yeast has been produced commercially in Europe for more than 150 years. Pure strains of this yeast, however, did not become available until the late 1800s. What is important to the baker is the yeast's ability to convert fermentable sugars (sucrose, maltose, dextrose, and fructose) into alcohol and the leavening gas carbon dioxide (CO_2). The carbon dioxide is not only useful for expanding the dough structure by inflating air cells formed during mixing within the three-dimensional gluten matrix, but it also dissolves in the dough moisture and forms carbonic acid, which lowers the pH of the dough. Later, in the crumb, the carbonic acid also contributes to the taste of the bread.

While about half of the alcohol formed by the yeast is lost during the baking process and most of the remaining alcohol is retained in the bread crumb, some of it enters into chemical reactions with organic acids produced by lactic acid bacteria or is oxidized by yeast enzymes to aromatic aldehydes. All these reaction products add to the unique bread flavor.

Fresh Yeast

Baker's yeast is available today in several different forms. The most popular kind is the *compressed yeast* (fresh yeast). It contains approximately 70% moisture, 15.5% protein and about 12-14.5% carbohydrates. If properly packaged and stored at 35-45°F (2-7°C), this type of yeast will retain its activity for about two weeks. Even though most bakeries were able to use yeast from different manufacturers interchangeably until the early 1970s, there may be significant differences in yeast performance today, particularly in sweet doughs. These differences are due to the selection of yeast strains and the conditions under which the yeast was grown by the manufacturer. These differences may become very critical in fully automated plants which do not allow for much variation in proof times, but may be of little significance to small retail shops.

Compressed yeast is also known in the baking industry as fresh yeast and is available as *crumbled yeast* in bulk packages and as *cake yeast* overwrapped in waxed paper. The cake yeast is preferred by smaller baking plants since it comes either in one-pound or five-pound (five one-pound units packaged as one block) "cakes," or packages, to facilitate the weighing process in these shops. While cake yeast has a fairly good tolerance and can be exposed to the ambient temperature in bakeries for up to 15 minutes, crumbled yeast must be kept refrigerated until it is used. Also, the container of the crumbled product should be kept closed tightly, even during short-term storage, to prevent fresh air from coming into contact with the ingredient. The presence of oxygen causes a rapid deterioration of yeast vitality.

While the crumbled yeast is generally used in a refrigerated water slurry to facilitate metering in automated batching systems for plastic and liquid ferments, most of the cake yeast is added directly to the mix, either crumbled up or "pasted" with (suspended in) some dough water. This type of yeast is readily incorporated into doughs and starts fermenting sugars immediately, even before the dough is fully mixed.

Cream Yeast

Compressed yeast is manufactured by concentrating *cream yeast* with a solids content of about 18% to a solids content of approximately 30%. Cream yeast has been made available to the baking industry in the United States only since the 1980s. The initial installation of a cream yeast system in a bakery can cost from $200,000 to $500,000 (Anonymous 1993) and is usually amortized with contracted purchases of the ingredient. Stored at the recommended temperature of 36°F (2°C) with slow agitation in the tank, cream yeast has a shelf-life of up to three weeks. It is used for the same applications and at the same solids level as compressed yeast. The recommended exchange ratio is:

1 lb. compressed yeast = 1.7 lb. cream yeast - 0.7 lb. water

Dry Yeast

Dry yeast is produced by extruding a special strain of compressed yeast through screen-like perforated plates. The strands are broken up, dried to a low moisture, ground, and packaged. Some dry yeasts are also blended with other additives to increase their stability and rehydration rate.

the baking industry as *active dry yeast* (ADY). It was developed in the 1940s in response to special needs during World War II. Unless ADY is to be stored for an extended period of time, it does not require refrigeration. If packaged under vacuum or in an inert atmosphere, active dry yeast has a shelf-life of up to two years. Its production combines a special strain of *S. cerevisiae* with specific growth conditions and a carefully controlled drying procedure. ADY has a relatively low protein content (38-42%) and a high level of carbohydrates (39-47%).

For best results, active dry yeast must be rehydrated in warm water before it is added to doughs or preferments. Yeast manufacturers recommend doing this with four to six parts of 100-110°F (38-43°C) water for every part of ADY. A rehydration time of 5-10 minutes at this temperature is generally adequate. Longer rehydration times may cause foaming, which is the result of destructive autolysis.

Dried yeast is rehydrated in warm water because, during the drying process, the cell membrane of yeast can become very porous. This process is reversed more quickly in warm water than in cooler water, which slows down the rehydration process. Cool water may also cause the leaching of up to half of the soluble components in the yeast cell, which include glutathione. Glutathione is a powerful reducing agent which not only reduces the mixing time, but also weakens the gluten structure in the dough. This can result in a significant reduction in loaf volume.

On a solids basis, active dry yeast has an activity equivalent to 65-75% fresh yeast. Therefore, for conversion from fresh yeast to ADY, a conversion factor in the range of 0.44-0.5 will give the desired results. This means that a baker should multiply the pounds (or ounces) of compressed or crumbled yeast he uses in his dough by this factor to calculate the amount of ADY needed to substitute for the fresh yeast. The same result may be obtained by using 7-8 oz. of ADY for every pound (16 ounces) of fresh yeast replaced.

A more stable form of ADY is *protected active dry yeast* (PADY). This type of yeast was developed in the 1960s (Anonymous 1993) as an ingredient for mixes. It has a lower moisture content and added antioxidants and emulsifiers. The emulsifiers facilitate the rehydration of the yeast and, thus, help reduce leaching from yeast cells.

The shelf-life of protected active dry yeast can be up to twice as long as that of the regular, unprotected form. Otherwise, there is no significant difference between them. The rehydration procedure and the use-levels are the same for both types of active dry yeast.

Another form of dry yeast was developed in the 1960s. It became known as *instant dry yeast* (IDY). This yeast was the result of a new strain of *S. cerevisiae*, of different growth and drying conditions, and the addition of emulsifiers. It is packaged under vacuum or in an inert atmosphere, and can have a shelf-life of one year at room temperature. Based on solids, its activity ranges from 80-90% of fresh yeast. This means that one pound (16 ounces) of fresh yeast can be replaced with 5.5 to 6.5 ounces of IDY, which is a ratio of 0.34 to 0.4 parts of IDY for every 1.0 part of fresh yeast.

Instant dry yeast has a moisture content of approximately 5%. A protein content of 43-44% in conjunction with about 40% carbohydrates not only assures that this dry yeast has a good activity in doughs, but also a very good stability during storage in the unopened package. However, once the package is opened and the instant dry yeast is exposed to oxygen in the air, the yeast's shelf-life is greatly reduced. The unused portion of instant yeast should always be stored under refrigeration and must be used within one week.

It is very important that the IDY is rehydrated either in warm water (86-110°F or 30-43°C) or during the mixing process by its addition to the flour. The very fine particle size of this yeast makes this possible in most doughs. Very dry doughs, such as bagel doughs, however, are an exception and may contain insufficient moisture to rehydrate the yeast during mixing. Regardless of the method of addition used, it is important to remember that IDY should never be added to cold water! The leaching of glutathione from yeast cells during improper rehydration can have a significant weakening effect on the gluten structure. At the same time, it also provides the potential benefit of a reduced mixing time for the dough.

In addition to the "regular" yeast varieties, yeast manufacturers make special yeasts available for specific applications, such as no-sugar doughs, high-sugar doughs, flavoring (inactive yeasts), and others.

Salt

Salt, although mostly thought of as a flavor enhancer, also helps control yeast activity and strengthens the protein matrix which forms the crumb structure of the bakery food. It is, therefore, of utmost importance that the salt is completely dissolved in doughs. Coarse salt, which is sometimes used in underdeveloped countries, should be dissolved in warm water before being added as a dough ingredient.

Since salt affects proteins, it also affects the gluten development in doughs. Even though it strengthens the gluten, salt also delays its formation during mixing. In order to reduce the total time required to mix a dough, many bakers add the salt after the gluten structure has started to develop. How late the salt can be added to doughs de-to develop. How late the salt can be added to doughs depends not only on how soluble the salt is, but also on how "dry" or "wet" and on how cold the dough is. Salt needs more time to dissolve in a stiff bagel dough than in a soft English muffin dough. But with most salt varieties used in bakeries today, two or three minutes of high-speed mixing are usually sufficient for this ingredient to dissolve and disperse in white pan bread and other soft doughs.

The delayed salt addition method is used primarily in large bakeries with tight production schedules. Small retail shops rarely use this time-saving procedure. In these bakeries, rather than working on a tight time schedule, the baker is generally involved simultaneously in a multitude of production processes so that it is easy to forget the late addition of salt.

Although salt is a relatively pure chemical (sodium chloride), it is sold in many different shapes and sizes. Most of the rock salt mined, and the solar salt produced by evaporation of sea water, is used by the chemical industry, for deicing roads, or for water treatment. According to the Salt Institute in 1992, only about 5% of dry salt produced is for human consumption, either directly or indirectly as part of processed foods.

The manufacturing process determines how fast the salt dissolves in doughs. The three major types of salt used by the baking industry are *granulated salt, dendritic salt* and *Alberger salt.* All are produced from heated brine solutions pumped from underground salt deposits. The three types differ primarily in the shape and density of the salt crystals.

Granulated salt is available in several grades, ranging from coarse and general purpose salt to flour salt, the type preferred by many bread bakeries. Pulverized salt is also available for almost instantaneous solubility.

Flaked salt, which is also known as compacted salt, is

made from granular (cubic) salt that is compressed into flat aggregates with a smooth surface. Because of its relatively large surface area, this type of salt is generally preferred for topping bakery foods, such as pretzels and breadsticks.

The use of dendritic salt in food manufacture is increasing in popularity. In this type of salt, the crystals are modified through the addition of 5-10 ppm sodium ferrocyanide, or *yellow prussiate of soda* (YPS), to the brine. The YPS interferes with the growth of an orderly and tightly packed salt crystal. Wherever the salt crystal incorporates a YPS molecule, a void forms which increases the crystal's surface area and reduces its density. Both of these changes in the physical structure of the salt crystal enhance its solubility.

Alberger salt is manufactured by a special grainer process. In this process the brine is super-heated under pressure to 290°F (143°C). The pressure is then quickly reduced in a series of steps. This causes moisture to "flash" off and the brine to cool to 226°F (108°C). As the salt crystals are then allowed to grow in open pans, they form a "hopper-shaped" crystal looking like a hollow quadrilateral (four-sided) pyramid with 89% more surface area than a cube-shaped crystal. This extra surface area enhances the solubility of the salt enormously. The Alberger salt is also known as *grainer salt* or *natural flake salt*. The salt is sifted, and as many as seven different mesh sizes are available to the food industry. The unique surface properties of the Alberger salt crystals also give this product very good adherence to food surfaces.

There is also a variety of specialty salt products available to the food industry. Iodized salt was introduced in 1924 and is generally sold directly to the consumer. It has from 0.006 to 0.01% potassium iodide added, which can dissociate over time. The free iodine formed during this process can adversely affect the color of food. This severely limits the use of iodized salt in commercially prepared products. However, the addition of very small amounts of sodium sulfite or sodium carbonate will stabilize the iodide in the salt and will minimize this problem.

Salt is also used as a carrier for enrichment, such as vitamins and minerals. This takes advantage of the fact that the amount of salt that can be added to food is self-limiting and lies in the range of 1.5-2.5% of the total flour weight in the formula. Most bakers use salt at the level of 2% of the flour weight. However, not very many bakers are taking advantage of this method to enrich their bread and other bakery foods. Unless the baker is willing to keep two types of salt in inventory, the baker is forced to enrich all the manufactured products and to keep their salt level the same with respect to the total weight of flour in the formula.

Bakers trying to avoid negative effects of this ingredient during mixing or fermentation can resort to *encapsulated salt.* During the encapsulation process, the salt is coated with partially hydrogenated soybean oil at the ratio of 85 parts salt to 15 parts fat. The fat melts during the baking process and releases the salt.

The consumption of high levels of sodium (salt contains 39% sodium) has been linked to hypertension in about 6-10% of the general population. The blood pressure in these "salt sensitive" individuals can be increased or decreased by the consumption of salt. Much effort has been spent on the complete or partial replacement of common salt (sodium chloride) with potassium chloride or with a blend of these two chloride salts. One commercially available product is a blend of equal weights of sodium and potassium salt. Both salts have a similar effect on yeast fermentation and dough properties. However, potassium chloride has a bitter and metallic taste, which most flavor panelists reject. Much of this bitterness, however, can be masked with other flavoring ingredients, especially in rich formulations.

Salt is subject to "caking" (lumping) at high relative humidities. Manufacturers, therefore, tend to add anti-caking additives to salt. Besides YPS, calcium silicate, tricalcium phosphate (TCP), and sodium silicoaluminate are used for this purpose.

Secondary Ingredients for Bread

Sugars

Sugars are simple carbohydrates. They are divided into two groups:

    1) Simple sugars or monosaccharides:
        Dextrose (Glucose)
        Levulose (Fructose)
        Galactose
    2) Disaccharides (Composed of two Monosaccharides)
        Maltose (Glucose-Glucose)
        Sucrose (Glucose-Fructose)
        Lactose (Glucose-Galactose)

Although the baker applies the term *glucose* primarily to corn syrup, especially to the "regular" 42 DE (**Dextrose Equivalence**) corn syrup, glucose is actually the chemical name of a simple sugar. Another name for glucose is *dextrose*, which indicates that a polarized light beam passed through a solution of this sugar is rotated to the right (*dexter* means "right"). Since bakers apply the term "glucose" to corn syrups containing between 18 and 29% water, the term "dextrose" is generally reserved for the dextrose monohydrate (one molecule of water attached to each dextrose molecule), which contains only 9.1% moisture.

Glucose (dextrose) is one of the two sugars in the three most common *disaccharides* listed above (*di* means two and *saccharides* are sugars). Glucose is also the basic building block for the common *polysaccharides* (*poly* means "many") which include starch, glycogen (a starch-like substance found in cells of animals), and cellulose. Since saccharides (sugars) are *carbohydrates*, these polysaccharides are also known as *complex carbohydrates*. While the human digestive system can easily metabolize (extract energy from) starch and glycogen, it is unable to do the same with cellulose. Such indigestible organic compounds are called *fiber*. Some fibers, like natural cellulose, are insoluble in water and are called *insoluble fiber*.

The Food and Drug Administration (FDA) defines the term "sugar" in two different ways. In ingredient statements "sugar" implies regular sugar (sucrose) only. Sweeteners derived from corn or other starchy sources, from milk, and from fruits have to be labeled accordingly as "corn syrup," "lactose," or "concentrated fruit juice." But for nutritional labeling, the Nutrition Labeling and Education Act (NLEA) of 1990 specifies that the chemical and nutritional definition of "sugar" must be used for the declaration of how much "sugar" is contained in one serving of the food. In this particular application all the different mono- and disaccharides are combined under the generic term of "sugar."

With the exception of the common sugar sucrose, all the previously listed sugars are *reducing sugars* and are able to "reduce" chemically the cupric ion in a Fehling solution to the insoluble cuprous ion. Under favorable conditions, such as dry heat, these reducing sugars react with protein in flour, milk, eggs, and other ingredients to form the flavors and color in the crust of bakery foods. This "browning reaction" is also known as *Maillard Reaction* and is a very important contributor to the taste of baked, toasted, and fried foods. Acidity and a high moisture content in the product tend to inhibit this reaction.

Sucrose

The two sources for regular sugar, or sucrose, are sugar cane and sugar beets. In the refined form, cane and beet sugar are over 99.5% pure sucrose and can be used interchangeably in all bakery foods. Although both of its components, glucose (dextrose) and fructose, which is also known as *levulose*, are *reducing sugars*, sucrose does not have the ability to chemically "reduce" the cupric ion in the Fehling solution to the insoluble cuprous oxide. Sucrose, therefore, does not react with amino acids during baking to form Maillard (browning) reaction products. Sucrose produces a crust color by a different mechanism. It is commonly known as *caramelization* and takes place at slightly higher temperatures than the Maillard reaction by dehydration and polymerization (*condensation*) of the sugar.

The enzyme *invertase* in yeast breaks the bond between the two sugar components in sucrose shortly after the yeast comes into contact with the sugar during mixing. Thus, the sugar "sucrose" is replaced in yeast-leavened doughs within a few minutes with dextrose and fructose, which are directly fermented by the *zymase enzyme system* in the yeast. The zymase breaks down (ferments) each monosaccharide component (dextrose and fructose) of the sucrose into two molecules of ethyl-alcohol (ethanol) and two molecules of carbon dioxide.

While about half of the alcohol produced by the yeast during fermentation is lost during the baking process, some of the remaining alcohol reacts with organic fermentation acids and forms esters, which add to the flavor of the baked product.

Although some bakeries still use sucrose in bread production, most large bread bakeries have replaced it with *42% high-fructose corn syrup* (42% HFCS).

Brown Sugar

Brown sugar is essentially a partially refined cane sugar (sucrose). It contains some residual molasses, which contributes a distinct flavor to the product. This flavor is also the reason why bakers add brown sugar to their dark variety breads, especially the wheat and multi-grain type breads. Application levels are usually between six and ten percent of the total flour weight.

Brown sugar contains between 2-5% moisture. For this reason, brown sugar is also classified as *soft sugar*. When brown sugar is allowed to dry out, the invert sugar in the molasses residue causes the sugar particles to bind together into a rock-like substance, especially when the sugar is compressed. Once this has happened, it is best to recondition the dried out sugar by slowly agitating the sugar and about 10% of its weight in hot water. This water, however, must be subtracted from other liquids added to the mix.

Brown sugar is available in three major categories: light, medium, and dark. A light brown sugar contains less molasses than a medium or a dark brown sugar and contributes less taste to the bakery food. Some bakers prepare their own medium brown sugar by blending 10 lbs. brown sugar molasses with 90 lbs. granulated sugar.

Brownulated Brand Brown Sugar (Domino Sugar) is a pure, free flowing brown sugar. It will not lump, is easy to use, and will produce the same results as regular brown sugar.

Dextrose

Dextrose was first commercially produced in 1921. For many years dextrose was also known as *corn sugar* because it was produced from corn starch. This term, however, is no longer in common use. Dextrose is available in various particle sizes ranging from granular to finely powdered. It is easily differentiated from regular sugar by the much more pronounced negative heat of solution. This is the cooling effect one experiences, when one allows this sugar to dissolve on the tongue.

Although an anhydrous (no moisture containing) form of dextrose is available for the pharmaceutical industry, bakeries usually use the monohydrate (one molecule of water associated with every molecule of dextrose), since the monohydrate is more economical to use on an equal solids content basis. However, it must be remembered that this ingredient consists of only 90.9% dextrose solids (fermentable sugar) and 9.1% moisture.

The solubility of dextrose decreases rapidly at temperatures lower than 77°F (25°C), which makes it an ideal topping sugar for bakery foods. The relative sweetness of dextrose is only about 70-80% of the sweetness of sucrose tested under the same conditions.

Dextrose is completely fermentable. However, when used in large amounts, unfermented dextrose tends to crystallize in the crumb and crust. This manifests itself as "sugar spots" in the crust and in a very firm and dry crumb. Contrary to claims made by some, dextrose is not a humectant in bakery foods! In fact, rather than keeping the crumb of a product moist, by forming the monohydrate, dextrose has a noticeable drying effect when added at significant levels to doughs and batters.

Corn Syrups

There are two major groups of corn syrup available to the baking industry:

Glucose corn syrups (CS).

High-fructose corn syrups (HFCS).

The acid hydrolysis process for the manufacture of glucose syrups was discovered in 1811. (Hydrolysis is composed of *hydro*, which means water, and *lysis*, which means splitting. Hence, acid hydrolysis implies the breaking down of a starch molecule into smaller components with water in the presence of an acid). The first production facility in the United States was built in 1831 with a capacity of 30 gallons of syrup per day. After 1873 corn syrups were routinely produced in this country. But it took another 100 years before sufficient quantities of *high fructose corn syrup* (HFCS) became available to the food industry.

Today, corn syrups are no longer manufactured by acid hydrolysis alone. Depending on the desired end product, corn syrups are now produced either with a combination of acid and enzyme hydrolysis, or with a combination of different enzymes.

Regular glucose corn syrups are generally characterized by their DE (dextrose equivalence) value. Regular corn starch has a DE equal to zero. On the other hand, when the starch has been fully converted to dextrose, this sugar has a DE of 100. Regular corn syrup (glucose) has a DE of 42. There are also glucose syrups available to the food industry with DEs up to 95. However, even though two syrups may have the same DE, this does not mean that they are alike. Depending on the type of enzymes used for the conversion, a 42 DE glucose syrup may be high or low in maltose. The same is true for the higher DE glucose syrups. Regardless of the composition of the glucose syrups, only the 95 DE corn syrup is economical for use in bread doughs. It must, however, be stored at a temperature above 122°F (50°C), or it will solidify quickly as a monohydrate. Lower DE corn syrups do not contain enough fermentable sugars to be useful in yeast leavened doughs.

Baker's yeast ferments only maltose (disaccharide: dextrose - dextrose), fructose, and dextrose. It is unable to metabolize starch fragments with more than two dextrose units (maltose) in the chain. While 97% of the solids in 95 DE corn syrup are fermentable, only about one third of the solids in 42 DE corn syrup can be utilized by the yeast. This increases to two-thirds of the solids in 62 DE corn syrup. Although these corn syrups are still available to, and are used by, the baking industry in a variety of bakery foods, only the 95 DE glucose syrup is, to a limited extent, used in the manufacture of yeast-raised bakery foods.

High fructose corn syrup (HFCS) became available to the food industry in the early 1970s. It is manufactured from demineralized 95 DE corn syrup which is passed through immobilized enzyme columns in which the enzyme *isomerase* converts (*isomerizes*) some of the dextrose to fructose. The end product of this process is 42% HFCS. The 42% in this descriptive name signifies that the solids in this syrup are comprised of 42% fructose sugar. The remaining solids are 50% dextrose and 8% maltose and higher sugars, i.e., three or more dextrose units per molecule. Further refining concentrates the fructose content in this syrup to 80 or 90%. The 55% HFCS is produced by blending appropriate amounts of 80 or 90% HFCS concentrate with 42% HFCS. Very little, if any, 55% HFCS is used by the baking industry; most is used by the soft drink industry.

Like the 95 DE corn syrup, the 42% HFCS contains 29% moisture which must be considered as dough water. Whereas the 42% HFCS can be safely stored at 90°F (32°C) with light agitation, the 95 DE corn syrup must be kept at a temperature of 122-127°F (50-53°C) until it is diluted to a lower concentration or added to the mix. While some of the dextrose in HFCS is eventually precipitated from the syrup when it is stored at normal temperatures found in bakeries, the 95 DE corn syrup will solidify at temperatures lower than 118°F (48°C). It is for this reason that most bakeries have discontinued using 95 DE corn syrup in their plants and have switched to 42% HFCS.

Malt

There are two major types of malt on the market, diastatic and non-diastatic. The *diastatic malt* contains diastase, an amylolytic enzyme system. These enzymes are intentionally inactivated by heat in the manufacture of *non-diastatic malt*. Each type of malt is available to the baking industry as viscous syrup or dry powder. There is no limitation to the amount of malt that can be added to bakery foods other than Good Manufacturing Practices (GMP) and economics. The functionality of diastatic malt products makes their use self-limiting.

Diastatic malt improves the "flow" characteristics of dough, i.e., it helps the dough pieces with spreading in the pan. The diastatic enzymes (amylases) in malt break down starch in the dough and convert it to fermentable sugars. These are primarily maltose and can be utilized by the yeast along with sugars added as part of the malt syrup or powder.

The diastatic activity of the enzymes in malt is expressed as degrees Lintner (°L). The higher the °L value, the greater the amylolytic activity of the malt and its ability to break down the starch into fermentable sugar and shorter starch fractions (*dextrins*). This makes diastatic malt an ideal ingredient for yeast-leavened doughs that have no fermentable sugar added. Non-diastatic malts are used solely for flavor and crust color in products in which amylolytic activity is not desired, such as crusty breads, rolls, bagels, and some cookies.

Besides the enzymatic activity in diastatic malt, both types of malt contribute the typical malt flavor and reducing sugars for the browning (Maillard) reaction. Malt products also add some color to bakery products. The main benefits, however, are found in the better color and flavor of the crust. Only at very high levels (5% of the flour weight or more) can malt be tasted in the crumb of breads. For this reason, malt is best used in products with high crust to crumb ratios, such as baguettes (French bread), hard rolls, and bagels. There is little benefit derived from the addition of malt to white pan bread doughs. Fungal alpha-amylase will do just as well in this application.

Malt is available in many different forms. *Malt extract* is extracted from malted barley and is offered to the food industry with a diastatic activity ranging from 0-400°L, with 20°L and 40°L syrups being the most popular types used in the baking industry. Dry extracts are also available, but only in the non-diastatic form.

Malt syrups are produced by adding corn grits to the barley mash. The enzymes in the barley mash act on the corn grits and thus produce additional fermentable carbohydrates. There are many different ratios of barley to corn available, which affect the price of these ingredients. The enzyme activity of these syrups ranges from 0-60°L. Dried syrups are non-diastatic.

Dry diastatic malts are produced from malted barley flour. Wheat flour and dextrose are added to standardize the malted barley flours to an activity of 20° or 60°L. Diastatic malt powders are recommended strictly for their enzymatic activity and are not used to improve the color or flavor of the crust of baked foods.

Molasses

Food grade molasses is a by-product of cane sugar production. Beet sugar molasses is not used in food products because of its inherent astringent flavor. Most beet sugar molasses is used either as animal feed, or as feedstock for yeast production.

After the cane juice is concentrated, the sucrose crystallizes and is removed from the syrup with a centrifuge. This process can be repeated several times. As more and more sugar is extracted from the syrup, the ash content of the molasses increases, the flavor becomes stronger, and its color becomes darker. The baker, therefore, differentiates between light (1.5-3% ash), medium (3-6% ash), and dark (7% or more ash) molasses.

Cane sugar molasses is classified into four basic grades:
Imported
Mill
Refiners Syrup
Blackstrap

The *imported molasses* originates outside the United States. It has a light and clear color and a delicate cane flavor. Most of it is imported from the West Indies.

Mill molasses is produced from domestically grown sugar cane. It has a harsher flavor and darker color than the imported molasses.

Refiners syrup is extracted from raw sugar during the refining process. It is light in color and is sweet. It lacks, however, the true molasses flavor characterizing the imported and mill molasses.

Blackstrap molasses is the leftover syrup after most of

the sucrose has been extracted from it. Although there are some edible "blackstrap" molasses available, these are really only dark molasses. The real blackstrap molasses is used either for animal feed or as feedstock for yeast production.

The baker generally chooses the type of molasses most suitable for the product. Blends of the edible types are also available.

Although liquid molasses contains between 65 and 75% sugar (almost half of it is invert sugar), it is used primarily for adding flavor to dark breads and other food items. Light, medium and dark molasses are also mixed with granulated sugar to produce brown sugar.

Molasses contains between 20 and 25% moisture. At these moisture levels the water activity of molasses is too low to support microbial organisms, i.e., molasses does not spoil easily. Sometimes, sugar refiners add small amounts of sulfur dioxide to molasses to further reduce the potential of a wild yeast fermentation.

Several types of molasses are also available in the dry form. These dry molasses have a residual moisture content of 1.5-4% of the total weight. Manufacturers of dry molasses usually recommend replacing liquid molasses with an equal amount of dry product and adding between 3-6 oz. of additional water per pound of dry molasses in the formula.

Honey

Honey is a natural syrup produced by the honey bee from the nectar secreted by flowers. There is no "Standard of Identity" for honey; but the United States Department of Agriculture (USDA) defines the standards for the various grades of extracted and comb honey. The moisture content for *Grade A Honey* and *Grade B Honey* cannot exceed 18.6%, while it can be as high as 20% for *Grade C Honey*. However, the average moisture content of commercial honey is about 17.1%. At this moisture content, honey has a specific gravity of about 1.42 at 20°C (about 12 lbs. per gallon) and a water activity of less than 0.6. Since all unprocessed honeys contain sugar-tolerant yeasts, pasteurization (treatment with heat to destroy microorganisms) is essential for a long shelf-life of this syrup. After pasteurization, the low water activity and a pH generally below 4.5 add to the microbial stability of honey.

About 0.5% of the honey is protein, amino acids, vitamins, and minerals. Except for the water, the remaining components are carbohydrates, mostly sugars. The approximately 38.5% fructose in honey makes this natural syrup an excellent humectant, especially in cookies. The 31% glucose has a tendency to crystallize during prolonged storage, especially at temperatures below 59°F (15°C). Less than 13% of the honey consists of disaccharides (maltose and sucrose) and trisaccharides or other carbohydrates. This makes honey an excellent source for fermentable sugars.

The organic acids and "source-specific contaminants" in honey give this ingredient its characteristic taste. Elevated storage temperatures and the presence of acids promote the formation of hydroxymethylfurfural (HMF) from simple sugars, such as glucose and fructose. With time, the furfurals darken syrups of these sugars and give them a bitter and undesirable taste. However, stored in airtight non-metal containers in a temperature range of 70-80°F (21-27°C), honey will remain in good condition for one year or slightly longer. Non-ideal conditions may reduce this time significantly.

Although most commercial honey sold in North America

is from clover fields, the more flavorful honeys come from wild flowers, shrubs, and tree blossoms, such as orange blossoms. Some of these honeys, like from buckwheat, are quite dark and may affect the color of the product made from this sweetener. While some of these special honeys demand a higher price and are used only in special applications or directly by the consumer, others may be less expensive.

Bread bakers use honey primarily to add flavor to their dark variety breads, epecially wheat and whole wheat breads. The honey is added, either by itself at levels normally ranging from 6-8% (f.b.), or in combination with another fermentable sugar. However, to get any benefit from the flavor of honey in bread, it must be used at a level of at least 4% of the flour weight.

Fats and Oils

Fats and oils are nature's answer to the need for storing energy in a concentrated form. The only difference between these two groups is their physical state. While fats are solid or plastic at room temperature, oils are liquid. In this discussion of the functionality of fats and oils, the term *fat* applies to all members of both groups, unless stated otherwise. It does not include mineral oil and other petroleum products.

Each gram of fat or oil contains approximately nine calories of energy. This compares to four calories per gram of protein or carbohydrates (starch and sugars).

In bakery foods, fats are used to "shorten" the texture of the crumb, i.e., to reduce the toughness of the crumb and the crust. Fat also tends to soften the crumb, which may then be perceived as "fresher." Fat is an excellent solvent for flavors and thus helps to retain some of these during baking. In sliced breads, the fat or oil in the crumb also helps to lubricate the slicing blades and prevents the build-up of a "gummy" deposit on the blades, which interferes with "clean" slicing.

Until about 1970, most bakeries used lard in bread. Lard was readily available and when the lard was rendered in open vats, rather than by steam, it also contributed a good flavor to the bread. However, meat fats (including lard) were found to not only contain relatively high levels of cholesterol, but also large amounts of saturated fatty acids, which are believed to cause a variety of human diseases. Therefore, an effort was made by the baking industry to replace lard and meat fat based shortenings with vegetable fats, which are generally a little more expensive, but usually contain less saturated fatty acids and no cholesterol.

Whereas bakeries used four to six pounds of shortening, butter, or margarine per 100 lbs. flour in bread doughs during the years following World War II, there is hardly a large bakery today using more than three pounds of a vegetable shortening per 100 lbs. flour. In fact, many bread bakeries today use only two pounds of soybean oil along with about one half pound of a dough strengthener and an equal amount of monoglycerides for crumb softening.

In addition to their main functions, the high melting point fat-like dough strengtheners and the crumb softeners also replace the hard fat portion formerly supplied by the lard or bread shortening. The hard fat is essential for lubricating the gluten structure for a good extensibility of the dough and also for a good gas retention during the early stages of baking. A non-hydrogenated vegetable oil does not provide these functions efficiently in bread doughs.

The use of two parts of soybean oil per 100 parts flour in bread doughs is now preferred by large bakeries, because the oil is not only cheaper than partially hydrogenated vegetable shortenings, but it can also be stored in bulk. An added benefit is that the cost for disposing packaging material is eliminated and that the storage tanks and piping to the mixers do not require heating. Oil can be metered accurately and automatically, is less objectional nutritionally, and it provides significant savings when used in place of 3% hydrogenated vegetable shortening. However, using a liquid vegetable oil without the addition of some form of hard fat is not recommended.

Milk and Milk Replacers

Until the late 1960s, *Nonfat dry milk* (NFDM) was used by bread bakers at the rate of four parts NFDM for every 100 parts of flour. Today, nonfat dry milk is rarely used by commercial bread bakers. A large assortment of milk replacers is now offered to the baking industry with a variety of claims.

The majority of milk replacers are based on whey, a cheap by-product of cheese manufacture. Whey supplies the reducing sugar lactose for good crust color development. The addition of soyflour with the whey not only provides the necessary protein for the browning (Maillard) reaction, but also increases the dough water absorption to the same level as NFDM. Many manufacturers of milk replacers, but not all, also formulate this ingredient to contain the same amount of protein (35%) as found in NFDM, to make the replacer nutritionally equivalent to milk solids. However, milk replacers vary significantly in composition, and the majority of them cannot be used interchangeably with another replacer, unless major changes in the ingredient and nutritional statements are made.

Bakers once added about 4% (f.b.) milk solids to their white pan bread in order to give it good toasting characteristics. Now the average bread baker adds only two pounds of a replacer instead. Although some bakers have also experimented with adding pure sweet whey to their doughs, most of them soon noticed that their doughs absorbed less water and, perhaps, also required more oxidation. Most hamburger bun manufacturers have discontinued the use of any dairy-derived ingredient without loss in product quality.

There is very little "milk bread" sold today. The standard of identity for milk bread requires either that all liquids are added as whole milk, or it must contain an equivalent amount of nonfat dry milk plus water and milk fat. Therefore, for a 60% (f.b.) dough water absorption, 8.2 lbs. of milk solids, including about 2.5-3.7 lbs. of pure butterfat, must be added per 100 lbs. of flour in the bread formula. No buttermilk, whey, or milk protein can be substituted for milk.

Eggs

Commercial bakers use eggs only in a few specialty breads, most of them of an ethnic origin. Even though many novice bakers believe that liquid whole eggs add moistness to their product, they are very disappointed when they find out that this is not the case. In fact, eggs tend to produce a tough crumb with a dry mouthfeel. To understand this, one only needs to think of hard boiled eggs! Unless one likes the egg flavor and the toughness eggs produce in the crumb structure, the use of eggs in yeast-raised bakery foods should be limited to ethnic breads and to those products which have to support extra weight from heavy fillings and toppings.

Fresh whole eggs are composed of approximately 65% egg white (egg albumen) and 35% yolk. The yolk contains all the fat in the egg (about 10.9% of the edible portion of whole egg or 34.1% of the yolk). Since the lecithin (an emulsifier) and cholesterol (a nutritionally undesirable fatty substance) are concentrated in the fatty portion of the egg, these substances are consequently found only in the yolk portion of the egg.

In order to call a product "egg bread" or "egg bun," it must contain at least one medium-sized egg per pound of bread or roll, or 2.56% dried whole eggs in the finished product (about 4 lbs. dried whole eggs per 100 lbs. flour). The Standard of Identity for egg bread is published in the Food and Drug Administration 21 CFR Part 136.

Fiber Ingredients

Most bakers try to combine a high content of dietary fiber in bread with a concurrent reduction in calories. This allows them to advertise high-fiber bread as "calorie reduced." In order to make this claim, the product's calorie content must be reduced at least 25% relative to the reference product, which is the standard product normally available to the consumer. But in order to call bakery foods "light" or "lite" in calories, the baker must reduce their caloric value by at least one third relative to the respective reference item. A claim of "low calorie" is almost impossible to meet with bakery foods. Such a product cannot contain more than 40 calories per 100 gram serving portion.

The food formulator is now able to choose from a vast assortment of food-fiber ingredients with varying levels of fiber content. Generally, insoluble fibers can be used at much higher levels in bakery foods than soluble fibers. Refined fiber ingredients are available at fiber concentrations ranging from 75 to 93%. There are essentially four major groups of fiber ingredients available to the food industry:

1) Cellulose fiber:
   Wood pulp
   Cottonseed lint
2) Bran fiber:
   Wheat bran
   Barley bran
   Corn bran
   Oat bran
   Soy bran
3) Cell wall material:
   Soy fiber
   Pea fiber
   Sugar beet fiber
   Fruit and citrus fibers
4) Vegetable, microbial, and marine gums:
   Seeds: Guar, locust bean
   Tree Exudates: Gum Arabic, karaya, traga-
   canth
   Microbial: Xanthan, gellan
   Cellulose gums: CMC, MCC
   Marine gums: Alginates, Carrageenan, Agar

While the cellulose fibers, bran fibers, and most of the cell wall material are composed primarily of insoluble fiber, the gums consist mostly of soluble fiber. Besides the fiber ingredients listed here, there are also others commercially available and used by individual bakers. With respect to calories, soluble fibers must be considered as complex carbohydrates with a calorie content of 4 kcal per gram.

When used at significant levels (5% or more of the flour weight), all fiber ingredients tend to have a detrimental effect on the loaf volume of bread. The magnitude of this effect varies with the type of fiber ingredient used and with the amount of water that must be added to obtain a pliable bread dough. Experience has shown that fiber ingredients absorbing not more water than 150% of their own weight tend to perform better in bread doughs than similar ingredients absorbing significantly more water. To overcome this loss in product volume, bakers usually add vital wheat gluten to their doughs at the level of approximately 0.4±0.1 lb. vital wheat gluten per pound of high-fiber ingredient with a 80-95% dietary fiber content.

Besides the loss in volume, abnormally high dough water absorption levels also tend to open the crumb grain and to produce a "tacky" crumb texture, while the extra wheat gluten imparts a slight toughness to the mouthfeel. Some fibrous materials also do not hydrate properly and give the crust a speckled appearance. Sometimes, but not always, this appearance can be minimized by adding the fiber ingredient to the preferment (sponge) instead of at the dough remix stage.

Of all high-fiber ingredients available, the cellulose fibers are the easiest to incorporate into food products. They are light in color and have neither taste, nor odor. At very high levels (over 20% of the total flour weight), however, they leave a dry mouthfeel, which many consumers characterize as "chalky." But overall, cellulose fibers show the least adverse effects in pan bread. An average cellulose fiber length of 35 microns was found to be most functional in bread and other yeast-leavened bakery foods.

The highly refined fibers from corn, peas, and soybeans are used by bakers who prefer not to use cellulose fiber manufactured from wood pulp or cottonseed lint. These fiber ingredients, however, tend to cause a slightly greater volume loss in bread. Some of these vegetable fibers may even noticeably affect the taste and crumb color of the bread.

Unless they are highly concentrated during the manufacturing process, brans are generally not as high in dietary fiber content as the highly refined cell wall material from legumes. Wheat bran has a dietary fiber content of about 42%, while oat bran contains only 16-18% fiber. The popularity of oat bran is primarily due to claims that the water soluble component beta-glucan has a cholesterol lowering effect in human blood serum. However, oat bran must not be confused with oat fiber, which is manufactured from oat hulls and contains no beta-glucan. Because of their relatively low fiber content, cereal brans are generally not suitable for lowering the caloric content of bakery foods to the "reduced" or "lite" level.

Most of the gums, no matter from what source, contain between 70-85% soluble fiber. Despite their high dietary fiber content, gums alone are not suitable for reducing the caloric content of bakery foods. Even though low levels (0.5 to 1.0% of the flour weight) of water soluble gums may increase the loaf volume of high-fiber bread, higher levels may lead to excessive expansion in the oven, followed by shrinkage, or even total collapse of the baked product during cooling.

High levels of gums change the rheology of doughs, too. The viscosity of the doughs increases so that more water must be added. This extra water makes the doughs difficult to process and the dough pieces become moist and "sticky." Therefore, only small amounts of gums (0.5-1% f.b.) should be added to yeast leavened doughs.

Vital Wheat Gluten

The first patent for vital wheat gluten was granted in 1939 in Australia. Even though this ingredient is now manufactured in the United States, much of it is still imported from Australia, Canada, and Europe. Although all vital wheat glutens have a protein content of 70 to 76%, the protein quality in wheat gluten can vary significantly with the wheat source and the drying conditions used during manufacture.

After the gluten has been "washed out" from a soft dough, it is dried to a moisture content of 6-8%. The drying conditions must be carefully controlled, so that the temperature of the protein is never raised above 140°F (60°C). At higher temperatures, the protein is "denatured," i.e., its ability to form a gluten matrix in a dough during mixing is destroyed (devitalized). The *vitality* of the wheat gluten can be checked by measuring the gluten's ability to "absorb" water. While a *vital wheat gluten* absorbs approximately 1.5-1.8 times its own weight in water, a *devitalized wheat gluten* (heat damaged gluten) absorbs very little water. Many researchers have searched for a simple test to determine the quality of vital wheat gluten. However, other than test-baking under realistic conditions, none of the chemical and physical test methods developed are able to predict the baking characteristics of gluten.

Most bakers using significant amounts of vital wheat gluten in their doughs like to add this ingredient to their plastic sponges. However, in cases where bakers use large quantities of wheat gluten, like in high-fiber breads, they generally add some of this ingredient (mostly amounts exceeding 5-6% of the total flour weight) at the dough remix stage.

Vital wheat gluten has the tendency to extend the dough mixing time slightly. The added wheat gluten does not seem to hydrate at the same rate as the protein in the flour. Some bakers even observed two distinct dough development peaks in high-fiber bread doughs made with high gluten levels. Although many doughs benefit from slightly longer mixing times, the second peak is not always obvious to the casual observer. It is generally recommended that the baker establish the optimum mixing time for doughs prepared with high levels of vital wheat gluten by experimentally increasing and decreasing the amount of mixing.

A shortage of vital wheat gluten in the United States during the mid-1980s produced a great effort to make vital wheat gluten more effective in bread doughs. The Japanese introduced an "enzyme activated wheat gluten," and others found that the performance of this ingredient was significantly enhanced by the addition of 0.5% (f.b.) DATEM (diacetyl tartaric acid esters of monoglycerides).

Vital wheat gluten is used to increase dough strength, for example, when the product requires a flour with a higher protein content than is available to the baker. Here, every pound of flour replaced with vital wheat gluten will have the effect as if the flour has a 0.6-0.7% higher protein content. This conversion factor will take into account a slight loss in the gluten vitality during drying. Thus, to upgrade an 11.5% protein bread flour to a 14% protein flour, one must replace about 4% of the flour with an equal amount of vital wheat gluten. At the same time, the dough water absorption is increased by approximately the same amount. However, when the vital wheat gluten is added to the flour (rather than used to replace part of the flour), 4% of this ingredient increases the dough water absorption by about 6%, or 1.5 lb water for every pound of vital wheat gluten added to the flour.

Vital wheat gluten is also used when the wheat flour is significantly "diluted" with a non-wheat ingredient or grain, such as a high-fiber product or rye flour. It is also added to strengthen the "hinge" of hamburger buns sold in the retail trade (1-2% of the flour weight), and to improve the volume of whole wheat bread (3-5% of the flour weight).

Raisins

Of all the dried fruits available to the food industry, raisins are the most popular variety. Raisins, if properly conditioned with water, provide not only a desirable taste and an attractive appearance, but they also add to the shelf-life of the product.

Thompson Seedless Raisins

About 97% of the California raisins are produced from Thompson seedless grapes. These grapes are harvested in late summer and are dried in the sun to a moisture content of about 12-15%. After processing and grading, the raisins are allowed to equilibrate and to reach a moisture content of about 18%. The raisins are then packaged and protected from drying out. At the ideal storage temperature of 45°F (7°C), raisins will keep for over one year. The low water activity of 0.55-0.62 for a moisture range of 15 - 18% protects the raisins from spoilage by microorganisms. Raisins also contain natural inhibitors, such as tartaric and propionic acids, which account for the relatively low pH (degree of acidity) of 3.5-4.0 and which contribute to the long shelf-life of raisin products.

The Thompson seedless raisins are offered to the baking industry in two sizes. Most bakers prefer to use the *Thompson midget raisins* (2200-2500 berries per pound) because their small size provides for a better distribution of the fruit in the baked product. The *Thompson select raisins* are slightly larger (1200-1500 berries per pound).

Each size of Thompson seedless raisins is available in three grades. *Grade A* has the highest percentage of matured berries and the lowest number of stems per pound. *Grade C* represents the lowest quality, i.e., raisins with the most defects.

Since raisins have the tendency to cling together when subjected to external pressure, free-flowing raisins were developed by coating the berries with a stable vegetable oil. The amount of oil added to these raisins ranges from 0.5-1.0% of the total weight.

Baking Raisins are preconditioned to a 25% moisture content and are free-flowing. They can be added directly to doughs and batters. This variety of raisins is available in sealed pouches to prevent loss of moisture and must be refrigerated after the container has been opened.

A new type of treated raisins became available in the early 1990s. These raisins are infused with glycerin, which keeps the raisins soft for a long time. Flavors can be added with the glycerin so that the fruit flavored infused raisins can take the place of various other fruits.

Bleached Raisins

Another variation of the Thompson seedless raisins is *bleached raisins* (golden raisins). These raisins are dipped into a mild caustic solution before they are washed with fresh water. The raisins are then treated with sulfur dioxide for bleaching, followed by mechanical drying.

Zante Currants

Although 97% of all raisins are manufactured from Thompson seedless grapes, the remainder of the raisins are produced from two other grape varieties. The *Zante Currants* are smaller grapes and were, at one time, preferred by bakers. The currants have a much higher count per pound than even midget raisins and thus have a better distribution in bakery products. However, currants are no longer readily available to the food industry. Even though before 1970 Zante Currants were lower priced than midget raisins, their scarcity now demands a premium price. Therefore, bakers use currants today only when the size of the midget raisins interferes with the proper distribution of raisins in the product or with the accurate scaling of the batter or dough.

Muscat Raisins

Another type of raisin rarely found in bakeries today is manufactured from the Muscat grape. *Muscat raisins* are very flavorful and are used in icings and specialty products. These raisins are quite large and they must be "seeded" (seeds removed) in order to make them acceptable to the general public.

Raisin Bread Standard

The Standards of Identity for raisin bread (Food and Drug Administration 21 CFR 136.160) requires that "not less than 50 parts by weight of seeded or seedless raisins are used for each 100 parts by weight of flour used."

Conditioning of Raisins

Since the water activity of the raisins is much lower than that of bread crumb, raisins tend to dry out the bread during and after baking, unless they are properly conditioned by soaking in water. During this process, the moisture content of raisins is increased from an average of 18% to about 25% of the raisin weight.

Bakers use many different methods for "soaking" raisins. Some of these methods are good, but some are not very beneficial to the end product. Bakers who soak raisins in excess water and then drain the water not absorbed by the raisins are not only wasting money, they are discarding the solubles of the raisins which are responsible for the sweetness and the distinct taste of this dry fruit.

Moreover, these bakers have no control over the amount of water added to the dough with the raisins, especially when they fail to control the temperature of the water and the time for soaking the dried fruit.

Since California raisins have been cleaned during processing, the best way to control the amount of extra water added to the dough is by soaking the raisins in a known amount of water. By adding all the water used for soaking the raisins, there are no losses incurred from leaching the raisins, and dough consistency is assured. A ratio of one part of 80°F (27°C) water for every four parts of raisins (4 ounces water per pound of raisins) always gives good results. This water should be poured over the raisins. When the raisins are leveled in the container and pressed down slightly, the water will reach the surface. After soaking for 30 to 45 minutes, there will still be some excess water in the container, which should be added to the dough with the soaked fruit.

Incorporation of Raisins into Dough

It is most important that the integrity of the raisins is preserved during mixing and processing of the dough. When the raisins have absorbed too much water during the "soaking" process, they tend to break up easily during mixing. But even properly conditioned (plumped) raisins will disintegrate during prolonged mixing. Therefore, raisins should be added to the dough at the very end of the mixing cycle, and they should be incorporated with a minimum amount of mixing. Excessive mixing will not only destroy the integrity of the berries, but it will also cause leaching of soluble components from the raisins. This includes organic acids, such as tartaric and propionic acid, which tend to interfere with yeast activity. Products made from these overmixed doughs will, therefore, require very long proof times and will lack oven spring (expansion in the oven during the early stages of baking) and volume.

Minor Ingredients for Bread and Rolls

Even though bakers call them *minor ingredients*, the term "minor" is not meant to imply that these ingredients are of a lesser importance for today's breadmaking technology. In fact, all of these ingredients have a significant effect on the general quality of bread and roll products.

Dough Conditioners

The term *dough conditioner* is not only used by bakers for ingredients which truly "condition" the dough, but also for combinations of ingredients with other functions in yeast leavened doughs. Many also use this term interchangeably with *(mineral) yeast food*. According to its descriptive name, the term "dough conditioner" should only be used for ingredients which truly *condition* the dough, i.e., improve dough processing characteristics for a better finished product quality.

Mineral Yeast Food

All "yeast food" contains a buffering salt, which helps to adjust the acidity (pH) in the preferment or dough. While the regular yeast foods are formulated with calcium sulfate, the acidic types contain monocalcium phosphate. The latter type of yeast food is preferred when the water in the bakery is very alkaline or when the baker wants to shorten the natural dough conditioning process, i.e., fermentation.

The true "yeast food" portion of the dough conditioner is the ammonium salt. Ammonium sulfate and ammonium chloride are being used interchangeably for this purpose. When used at the level recommended by the manufacturer, the yeast food will usually contribute about one ounce ammonium salt per 100 lbs. flour (0.0625% of the flour weight). The ammonium salt is added to yeast leavened doughs to provide a nitrogen source for the reproduction of yeast cells. It is not required for the fermentation process. Although bakers no longer depend on the reproduction of yeast cells in bread doughs during the bulk fermentation stage, and the count of yeast cells during this time is generally not increasing, it has been found to be beneficial to the final product quality when a small amount of an ammonium salt is added to the preferment.

Another commonly found component in "mineral yeast food" is an oxidizing agent. This oxidizing agent facilitates the formation of intermolecular disulfide bonds, which are required for a strong and stable gluten matrix. Most flours produce larger loaves with a better crumb texture when a small amount of one or two oxidizing agents is added to the flour preferment.

Until about 1991, the preferred oxidizing agent in mineral yeast foods was *potassium bromate*. At the recommended level of 0.5% (f.b.) yeast food, this ingredient contributed usually about 14 parts of potassium bromate per million parts of flour (ppm). Today, however, there are many "yeast foods" available to the baking industry in which the potassium bromate has been replaced with other oxidizing agents (mostly ascorbic acid and/or azodicarbonamide), enzymes, and/or other "bread-improving" ingredients.

Oxidizing Agents

Ascorbic acid is also known as *vitamin C*. However, the vitamin C functionality of ascorbic acid is lost during dough processing and baking. Therefore, ascorbic acid in baked foods cannot be listed or claimed as vitamin C.

Even though potassium bromate, ascorbic acid, and *azodicarbonamide* (ADA) fulfill similar functions in yeast leavened doughs, the mechanisms and speeds of their reaction differ significantly. While the majority of the potassium bromate molecules are simply "reduced" to potassium bromide by giving up oxygen atoms, the azodicarbonamide removes the hydrogen atoms from the sulfhydryl groups (-SH) on wheat protein molecules, so that two sulfide groups can form intermolecular disulfide linkages (-S-S-). The bromate reduction to bromide is rather slow and is accelerated as the pH in the dough decreases and the dough temperature rises in the proof box and during baking. The ADA reaction, however, takes place very quickly and is probably completed shortly after mixing by conversion of the ADA to biurea. Although the added potassium bromate is generally listed in the ingredient statement, azodicarbonamide is considered a processing aid and it is assumed that the finished baked product contains no trace of this additive. Neither the ADA, nor the biurea are known to be a threat to human health.

The ascorbic acid behaves entirely differently from potassium bromate and azodicarbonamide in doughs. Ascorbic acid is actually a reducing agent in the absence of air (oxygen). It is, therefore, not a suitable oxidizing agent for "closed systems," such as continuous mixers. However, in conventional mixers operating under atmospheric conditions, enzymes oxidize the ascorbic acid rapidly to dehydroascorbic acid (DHAA), which will then gradually oxidize the sulfhydryl groups in the flour protein by absorbing the hydrogen atoms from the sulfhydryl (-SH) groups, like the ADA does very rapidly. The rate of reaction of ascorbic acid is slower than that of ADA, but faster than of potassium bromate.

Another oxidizing agent available to the baking industry is *potassium iodate*. This additive has specific applications and it is not in widespread use. The iodate functions similarly to the bromate, except that the reaction takes place almost immediately after the iodate comes into contact with flour and water. *Calcium iodate* and *calcium bromate*, too, have found specific applications in the United States food industry and are not part of a bakery's "normal" ingredient inventory.

The legal maximum limit for the use of ADA in doughs in the United States is 45 ppm of the total flour weight, including the ADA added to the flour at the mill. The maximum legal limit for bromates, iodates, and calcium peroxide combined is 75 ppm of the total flour weight. However, the use of potassium bromate in bakery foods is no longer allowed in Australia, Canada, and most European and Asian countries. Use of potassium bromate in the United States is also increasingly restricted.

Because of the differences in their reaction rates, each oxidizing agent functions slightly differently in yeast-leavened doughs. Substituting one for another will often give different results, unless other formula adjustments are also made.

Because the oxidizing agents are used in such small amounts, bakeries usually buy and use them in tablet form. The amount of the specific oxidizing agent added with each tablet per 100 lbs. flour is generally stated as parts per million parts of flour.

Dough Drying Agent

Calcium dioxide (also known as *calcium peroxide*) is an excellent dough conditioning agent for soft doughs with a high dough water absorption. When used at the level of 27 to 35 parts of calcium dioxide per million parts of flour, it is claimed that up to three pounds of additional water can be added to the dough without causing "stickiness" or difficulties during dough processing. Because this ingredient is used in such small amounts, it is generally sold and used in combination with other ingredients.

Calcium dioxide reacts with other ingredients in the mix as soon as it comes into contact with moisture. This dough drying ingredient must, therefore, be added directly to the mix at the final mixing stage. It must never be added with other ingredients in a water slurry, especially not when this slurry contains reducing agents, like L-cysteine, or ascorbic acid.

Reducing Agents

Reducing agents have the opposite effect in doughs from oxidizing agents. Whereas the latter facilitate the formation of intermolecular disulfide linkages (-S-S-), reducing agents interfere with this process. The most frequently used reducing agent in white pan bread is *L-cysteine*, an amino acid. L-cysteine (CYS-H) is the same amino acid which, as a component of gluten proteins, produces the intermolecular bonds between neighboring protein molecules.

Bakers like to use L-cysteine to reduce mixing times and to increase the extensibility of doughs. However, its use is limited to "no-time" doughs and is rarely used in sponge or liquid ferment doughs.

The chemical reduction is generally accomplished when one of two exposed sulfide radicals of a broken intramolecular disulfide bond (RS-SR broken by kneading action to form RS- + RS+) accepts the hydrogen ion H+ (a *reduction reaction*) from the L-cysteine molecule (RS- + H+ = RSH), while the remaining part of the cysteine molecule (CYS-) forms a disulfide bond with the other member of the broken disulfide bond (RS+ + CYS- = CYS-SR). By preventing the reformation of intramolecular disulfide bonds (disulfide bonds within the same molecule), the gluten proteins will "develop" more quickly into gluten. But, unless a slow acting oxidizing agent is also added, these chemically reduced doughs tend to be weak in structure, and the resulting bread will tend to have a more open grain with a coarse texture. The presence of oxidizing agents will facilitate the reformation of disulfide bonds, but instead of within the same molecule (intramolecular), the new bonds will form primarily between different molecules (intermolecular).

Bakers who do not like to use L-cysteine as an ingredient in their breads may use deactivated dry yeast instead. Dead yeast cells contain the tripeptide (three amino acids bonded together to form a peptide) *glutathione*. While one of the three amino acids is glutamic acid which is also one of the amino acid constituents in wheat gluten, the amino acid in the middle of the tripeptide is L-cysteine. The L-cysteine in this tripeptide is as functional as the L-cysteine added to doughs by itself, i.e., it is a powerful reducing agent and dough relaxer.

Another functional reducing agent is deodorized garlic, which is available to the food industry in two different concentrations. If used as recommended, this natural dough conditioner will impart no noticeable garlic taste to the baked product.

Enzymes

Although fungal enzymes are used in bakery products for many different reasons, many bakers add extra enzymes strictly for conditioning their doughs. Generally, enzymes are favored by warmer dough temperatures. Their activity increases by about 40% for every 10°F (5.5°C) increase in dough temperature. However, one must keep in mind that fungal enzymes are rapidly inactivated at temperatures above 150°F (65°C). Enzymes derived from cereal grains are slightly more resistant to heat, even though none of them survive the baking process. Enzymes continue to facilitate specific reactions until they are deactivated either by heat or by changes in the substrate, such as water activity, acidity, reaction products, etc. Most of all, one must keep in mind that enzymatic actions are not reversible!

Application levels for enzymes vary with the magnitude of the desired effect, the temperature of the dough or ferment (substrate), and the length of time the enzymes are allowed to act upon the substrate. While warmer temperatures tend to have a positive effect on enzyme activity, refrigeration inhibits most enzymes.

Amylases

Flour naturally contains an adequate amount of *beta-amylase*. This enzyme splits maltose molecules (two dextrose units combined as a disaccharide) from unbranched segments of damaged starch molecules and thus provides fermentable sugar for the yeast. This enzyme, however, is unable to break down branched portions of the amylopectin in the starch granules. This is accomplished by *alpha-amylase*. This enzyme attacks starch molecules in broken granules at random places and thus is able to convert even the branched amylopectin into shorter segments (dextrins) for further breakdown by the beta-amylase.

Soluble dextrins (3-9 dextrose units) were found to inhibit the firming process in aging bread crumb. Special amylase enzymes are now available to the baking industry as very effective crumb softeners.

Although many bakers buy *malted flour* with a specified amount of alpha-amylase activity, they may want to add additional *fungal alpha-amylase* to some doughs to provide more "flow" (spread) for the product in the proof box. Others add these enzymes to doughs formulated with very little or no sugar, so that the amylase can produce additional fermentable sugars for the yeast. These sugars also contribute to the crust color of the baked product.

Proteases

Bakers using very tough and strong flours, such as clear and high-protein flours, like to "mellow" the protein with *fungal protease* enzymes, which "cut" the long protein chains of amino acids at random into shorter segments for a more extensible dough. In order to reduce the mixing time of these "tough and strong" flours, the protease enzymes must be added to the preferment since at "normal" dough temperatures these enzymes tend to work on the flour protein rather slowly. In cases where no preferments are used and an immediate reduction in the mixing time is desired, the baker may use a very fast acting protease manufactured from a plant source, such as *papain* or *bromelain*. However, the baker must remember that these enzymes keep breaking down the gluten protein, until the product is almost baked. It is for this reason that most bakers shy away from using these powerful plant enzymes for reducing their dough mixing times.

Lipoxygenases

Another type of enzyme commonly used by the baking industry is the *lipoxygenase* found in enzyme-active soy flour. This enzyme acts on linoleic acid and forms fatty acid hydroperoxides with oxygen absorbed from the air. The resulting reaction product has not only a gluten strengthening effect, which increases the mixing tolerance of the flour, but it also oxidizes (bleaches) the carotenoid pigments in the flour. Some bakers even claim an improved taste in white pan bread made with enzyme-active soy flour, the primary source for lipoxygenase in bakery foods.

The Standards of Identity for white pan bread (21 CFR 136.110) allow the addition of ground dehulled soybeans (with or without oil removed) with enzyme activity of "not more than 0.5 part for each 100 parts by weight of flour used." The addition of approved food ingredients to non-standardized breads and other bakery foods is governed by *Good Manufacturing Practices*, which limit the level of their addition to not more than what is necessary to achieve the desired effect.

Dough Strengtheners

As bakers started to use bread flours with lower protein and higher ash contents, the addition of dough strengtheners grew in importance. All these dough strengtheners are classified as *emulsifiers*, although only few emulsifiers are really dough strengtheners. Emulsifiers, or surfactants, are generally defined as agents which reduce the surface tension of two normally immiscible components so that they can form an intimate and stable mixture. The term *surfactant* is applied to substances containing a hydrophilic (water-loving) and a lipophilic (fat-loving) component in their molecule. The lipophilic portion usually consists of a common fatty acid. The hydrophilic component is either a polymer of an ether (polyoxyethylene), a polyalcohol (glycerol), or any other oxygen containing organic component able to form hydrogen bonds with water molecules.

A close examination of the molecular structure of dough strengtheners indicates that dough strengtheners tend to be more hydrophilic than lipophilic, while crumb softeners appear to be more lipophilic than hydrophilic. However, the mechanism of "dough strengthening" is even less well understood than all the factors affecting crumb softness.

The most commonly used dough strengtheners for yeast-leavened doughs are:

Polysorbate 60

Ethoxylated monoglycerides

Succinylated monoglycerides

Calcium stearoyl lactylate

Sodium stearoyl lactylate

Diacetyl tartaric acid esters of monoglycerides

While the polysorbate 60, the ethoxylated monoglycerides (EMG), and the succinylated monoglycerides (SMG) are strictly dough strengtheners, the calcium and sodium stearoyl lactylates (CSL and SSL) and the diacetyl tartaric acid esters of monoglycerides (DATEM) have not only dough strengthening characteristics, but they also have a crumb softening effect. Because of the synergistic (enhancing) effect of some of the dough strengthening agents, they are often sold and used as blends with other dough strengtheners in this group.

The effectiveness of these ingredients depends on how well they are dispersed in the dough. If, for instance, the stearoyl lactylate is stored in a rather warm warehouse during the hot summer months, it is possible that the particles will soften and compact under physical pressure to form lumps, which will not break up and disperse properly during dough mixing. This will then reduce significantly the effectiveness of this ingredient. For this reason, it is very important that the baker follows the manufacturer's instructions for storing dry ingredients. Also, to assure maximum dispersion of these dry ingredients, it is recommended that, whenever possible, they be added to the preferments, i.e., sponges and liquid flour ferments.

Crumb Softeners

There are essentially two types of crumb softeners used by the baking industry. One type is the traditional lipophilic emulsifier, which has been in use for about a half century. The second type, enzymes, has a relatively short history, but an excellent potential.

The lipophilic crumb softeners are generally more difficult to incorporate into doughs than the more hydrophilic dough strengtheners. To make matters worse, the most effective crumb softeners also have high melting points. Although new technologies exist which make the addition of these ingredients to doughs possible in the powdered or granular form, the most efficient way to add them to doughs is either dispersed in fat or as an emulsion (aqueous dispersion).

Emulsifiers used as crumb softeners are of the following types:

Monoglycerides
Diacetyl tartaric acid esters of monoglycerides
Calcium stearoyl lactylate
Sodium stearoyl lactylate

Monoglycerides

Research has shown that monoglycerides of high melting point saturated fatty acids, particularly stearic acid, are more effective crumb softeners than the softer monoglycerides manufactured from unsaturated fats. Because of the difficulty of adding these hard monoglycerides directly to doughs, many ingredient suppliers make them available as emulsions with about three parts of water for every part of monoglyceride. This combination results in a plastic and fat-like paste, which can easily be weighed and added to doughs.

Staling Process

One mechanism by which monoglycerides retard "staling" (firming) of the crumb is relatively simple. But this mechanism does not fully explain the crumb softening effect of lactylates and diacetyl tartaric acid esters of monoglycerides (DATEM).

The staling process in baked products has been partially explained with *starch retrogradation*. This process is the change of starch in the crumb from an amorphous, random arrangement of starch molecules, to a tightly ordered crystalline state. Like water freezes, and sugar and salt crystallize when saturated solutions are cooled down, the process of starch retrogradation accelerates at lower storage temperatures. This process stops when the starch molecules are "frozen in place" at temperatures below about 5°F (-15°C).

Like many other crystals, the starch crystals "bind" (occlude) moisture. Since the starch molecules are tightly packed in the crystal, retrograded starch (stale crumb) loses its resilience and the product becomes firm. At the same time, as the moisture is occluded in the crystal, the product is perceived to be not only "dry," but also "tasteless," because the occluded moisture also contains the water soluble flavor components in the baked product. Therefore, a stale baked product is not only firm, but it also tastes dry and lacks the flavor and aroma of freshly baked goods. The staling process can be partially reversed by heating (toasting) the "stale" product. Heat will "melt" the starch crystals and allow them to return to a semi-random arrangement, thus temporarily reversing the staling process.

It has been found that monoglycerides "complex" with starch molecules, i.e., the monoglyceride attaches itself to a starch molecule. Since the monoglyceride molecule does not fit into an orderly and tightly packed arrangement of starch molecules in a crystal, it tends to slow down starch retrogradation. However, there is no indication, that other types of chemical crumb softeners use this same mechanism of complexing with starch.

Although there is no longer a legal limit to how much monoglyceride can be added to white pan bread doughs, all other dough strengthening and crumb softening emulsifiers can be used in white pan bread and rolls only at a maximum level of 0.5% of the total flour weight, either alone or in any combination. However, these restrictions do not apply to non-standardized bakery foods, which are governed solely by Good Manufacturing Practices.

Antistaling Enzymes

Much work has been done with bacterial alpha-amylases to control the staling process. The alpha-amylase randomly cuts (hydrolizes) the bond between two adjacent dextrose units in starch, thus producing smaller segments (dextrins) of the molecule. These smaller sections tend to weaken the otherwise rigid starch crystal. Since the bacterial amylase is usually not totally inactivated during the baking process, a small but significant amount of the enzyme continues to break down the starch in the crumb of the stored product. If this is not properly controlled, the mouthfeel of the product finally becomes "gummy," as more and more of the starch is reduced to shorter and shorter fragments. For this reason, bacterial amylases were never fully accepted by the baking industry. Manufacturers of enzymes have, however, found some very effective bacterial amylases which do not survive the baking process and which keep yeast-leavened products soft and fresh without developing gumminess. These bacterial enzymes tend to nearly arrest the crumb firming process three days after baking and are now available from several sources.

Preservatives

The term *preservative* is used in many different ways. To some, preservative means that it will prevent any change in eating quality (staling) or stop the deterioration of product appearance, such as the breakdown of icings and glazes. To most bakers, the function of a preservative is merely to prevent microbial spoilage in general, or mold growth specifically.

In order to properly understand the problem of preserving bread and other yeast-leavened products, the following important facts must be understood:

1) Bread is free of viable mold and mold spores when it leaves the oven. All mold growth is caused by post-bake contamination with viable mold spores.

2) All agents, chemical or natural, having an adverse effect on mold and other undesirable organisms will also have an adverse effect on yeast and other desirable organisms, i.e., they will slow down the fermentation and proof processes.

3) All preservatives only inhibit (slow down) mold growth. They do not prevent mold growth! The mold-free time period for a bakery product is more influenced by the extent of the post-bake contamination, than by the amount of a preservative added to the dough or batter, i.e., a heavily contaminated loaf of bread will have a very short shelf-life, regardless of the amount of preservative added to the dough!

One immediately recognizes the fact that there is no better "preservative" than the prevention of a post-bake contamination of the product with mold spores. The most critical time for a loaf of bread is the time after it has cooled to about 160°F (70°C) and before it is packaged. A fan blowing outside air over the cooling bread, especially on a humid day, guarantees a short shelf-life. Flour dust, dirty cooling racks, and unwashed hands or gloves are also frequent causes for product contamination with mold spores. Common sense and a good sanitation program are the most important preservatives for bakery foods. Chemical preservatives can only lend additional "support" to the effort to slow down mold growth by reducing "opportunities" for contamination with mold spores.

Propionates

Although there is a wide selection of chemicals approved for food application, most of them are not suitable for use in yeast-leavened products because they have a detrimental effect on yeast activity. Good Manufacturing Practices are the only restriction to their legal use. *Propionic acid* and its calcium salt are the most commonly used preservatives in yeast-leavened products. These chemicals have only a slight inhibiting effect on yeast fermentation when used at the recommended level of 3-5 oz. per 100 lbs. flour (0.19 -0.32% f.b.). At higher application levels, propionic acid and *calcium propionate* impart a distinct acid taste to the baked food. Both ingredients are also very effective against spoilage caused by *rope*. Propionates are most effective at pH levels below 5.5. Yeast-leavened products usually fall into the pH range of 5.2-5.5.

Rope is caused by heat resistant spores of the *Bacillus mesentericus* variant *B. Subtilis*. This bread disease is very infectious and causes spoilage of the crumb rather than of the crust. Rope is much more prevalent today than it was during the 1950s and the 1960s. It is most commonly found in moist bread made from stone-ground whole wheat. *Ropy bread* can be detected by its very moist crumb and by the odor of a ripe cantaloupe. This bread disease is named after sticky fine threads formed when a ropy product is pulled apart. These threads become visible when a bright light shines on them.

Sodium Diacetate

Sodium diacetate is another chemical preservative for bread products. Before ingredient labeling became mandatory during the early 1970s, many large bread bakeries used this preservative interchangeably with calcium propionate in the common belief that this change would prevent the adaptation of mold to one particular inhibitor. However, ingredient labeling makes it difficult to change from one ingredient to another, and most bakers now use only calcium propionate as a chemical preservative in their bread products.

Sorbic Acid and Postassium Sorbate

Sorbic acid and its salt potassium sorbate are not suitable for use in yeast leavened doughs since these inhibitors suppress yeast activity. However, a *5% potassium sorbate solution* in water can be sprayed on product as it leaves the oven. This method is quite effective against mold growth, since the preservative is concentrated on the surface of the product, where recontamination with mold spores takes place. Sorbic acid and potassium sorbate are effective at pH levels up to about 6. At higher pH levels the effectiveness of these preservatives decreases significantly.

Vinegar

Next to salt, *vinegar* has probably been used more and for a longer time as a preservative than any other food additive. Bakers add up to 1% (f.b.) of a 200 grain (containing 20% acetic acid) vinegar to their bread doughs. However, at this level the vinegar imparts a slight acidic aroma and a distinct taste to the bread. Like propionates, vinegar has only a relatively mild inhibiting effect on yeast activity.

Raisin Juice

Anyone who has ever mixed doughs with "plumped" raisins (raisins heavily soaked in water) knows that broken up raisins will not only discolor the dough, but the raisins will also interfere with yeast activity. It is rare that raisin bread spoils because of mold growth. These observations have prompted processors of raisin products to extract a *raisin juice concentrate* (Fagrell 1992) from soaked raisins and some bakers are now using this concentrate as a "natural preservative" in dark variety breads. The inhibiting ingredient in this concentrate is tartaric acid (2% concentration). The raisin juice concentrate also contains about 65% reducing sugar and about 29% moisture. Its natural dark color precludes the concentrate's use in white breads, when used at the recommended level of 2 to 4% of the flour weight.

Fermentation Products

Fermentation products of flour doughs and of whey are another category of natural preservatives. Special bacterial cultures are employed in the manufacture of high concentrations of organic acids to inhibit mold growth in baked bread with minimal inhibiting effect on yeast activity before baking. The end products of these two processes are carefully dried, ground into fine flours, and standardized to specified "strengths," i.e., concentration of inhibiting acids. One type of product is offered to the baking industry as a *Natural Dried Cultured Wheat Flour*, while the others are cultured whey products. These whey-derived natural preservatives are usually sold as *milk replacers* and are labeled as *Dry Sweet Whey and Cultured Sweet Whey*. Usage levels vary from less than 1% (f.b.) for the cultured wheat flour to up to 2.5% (f.b.) for the milk replacers.

Even though the active ingredient in cultured whey is propionic acid, these cultured products are not declared as "preservatives."

Labeling of Preservatives

Synthetically produced chemical mold inhibitors in bakery foods must be listed by their "common" name and their intended function must be declared. An example would be: "...calcium propionate (to retard spoilage)..." (Vetter 1993). Ingredients having a natural function as mold inhibitors do not need to be declared as preservatives. Vinegar and cultured whey or flour belong to this category of ingredients.

Modified Atmospheric Packaging

Another method used to control microbial activity on the product surface is to deprive the organisms of a substance vital to their survival. This is done with *modified atmospheric packaging* (MAP). There are two different means to accomplish this:

1) Displacing the air in the package with a mixture of gases, such as nitrogen diluted with 40-60% carbon dioxide. The oxygen level in the modified atmosphere should not exceed 1% of the total gas.

2) Absorption of oxygen in the package by an active material, such as iron filings, which oxidizes rapidly in the presence of moisture in the atmosphere.

These active materials are contained in gas-permeable packets and, if properly sized, reduce the oxygen content in the package to 0.01%. Although not edible, the sachets (sealed pouches) are non-toxic and impart no odor or taste to the product. However, one must keep in mind that the "effective life" of the packets is very limited, once they are removed from their protective container.

Another unique way to modify the atmosphere in the package is the use of a sachet filled with micro-encapsulated food-grade alcohol. However, this system is supposed not to function well for products with a water activity over 0.85. This fact, of course, limits the use of this product to foods with a relatively low vulnerability to mold growth. However, the user of any form of modified atmosphere packaging must not forget that the effectiveness of this preservation measure is only as good as the package itself, i.e., the ability of the film to retain its modified atmosphere and to exclude gases from the external environment.

Experimental Formulations

Introduction

The following formulations for white pan bread and hamburger buns are basic and may be altered to meet more specific needs or bread-making technologies used by a bakery or a baking ingredient supplier. For instance, a baking laboratory may want to use a particular milk replacer in the test baking formulation, because this ingredient is in inventory and in general use. If this is not the case, then it is better to use a more standard ingredient, like nonfat milk solids. Milk replacers often have unique functionalities in bakery foods not common to all milk replacers. Granulated sugar may be used interchangeably with 42% high-fructose corn syrup, as long as the 29% water in the syrup is taken into account. Dextrose monohydrate (about 9% moisture), too, is a very good fermentable sugar.

Depending on the objectives of experimental baking, it is usually best not to add dough conditioning enzymes and improving agents, such as sodium stearoyl lactylate (SSL), diacetyl tartaric acid esters of monoglycerides (DATEM), ethoxylated monoglycerides (EMG), etc. to experimental formulations used for the evaluation of other ingredients. These agents may mask some adverse effects of the test ingredients. Crumb softeners, such as monoglycerides, may be used, provided they do not interfere with the study of the effectiveness of another shelf-life extending test ingredient.

For simplicity, it is recommended that a non-bromated mineral yeast food is used in the formulation. This ingredient may be replaced with the proper proportions of its components: calcium sulfate or monocalcium phosphate, ammonium chloride or ammonium sulfate, and an oxidizing agent, such as ascorbic acid or azodicarbonamide (ADA).

Most partially hydrogenated shortenings contain between 21 and 25% saturated fatty acids and a similar amount of this fat is in the solid state at room temperature. These fat crystals are very important in bread manufacture since they improve the gas retention of the dough during proofing and the early stages of baking. In contrast, liquid vegetable oil contains no significant amount of fat crystals and is, therefore, not able to function in all aspects like a regular plastic shortening in bread doughs.

If the baker or baking technologist chooses to replace the partially hydrogenated bread shortening with a regular vegetable oil, it may become necessary to add either a small amount of hard fat or a high melting point fatty acid containing surfactant, like sodium stearoyl lactylate (SSL) or diacetyl tartaric acid esters of monoglycerides (DATEM). These emulsifiers also function in doughs like the hard fat in shortenings.

Instant dry yeast (IDY) may be used in place of compressed yeast. To make this conversion, multiply the amount of compressed yeast by a factor of 0.4. Thus, a formulation requiring the addition of 3 pounds of compressed yeast will produce the same results with 1.2 pounds of IDY.

$$3 \text{ lb.} \times 0.4 = 1.2 \text{ lb.}$$

When making this conversion, the baker or baking technologist may consider a slight increase in the amount of water added to the dough. This amount should equal the difference in the weight of the two yeasts:

$$3 \text{ lb.} - 1.2 \text{ lb.} = 1.8 \text{ lb.}$$

Because IDY contains a small amount of the powerful reducing agent glutathione, the dough mixing time may have to be slightly reduced.

Even though IDY retains its functionality in the unopened package for about one year when it is stored at "room temperature" or in a cool environment, it will deteriorate very rapidly once it comes into contact with oxygen from the air. An opened package of IDY must be stored in a closed container under refrigeration and should be used within five days.

Conversion of Weights

Bakers who prefer to work with pounds (lb.) and ounces (oz.) instead of grams (g) and do not have a McDuffee bowl available, may convert the following formulations to suit their needs by dividing the grams by 20 if they want to use a 20 quart mixing bowl, or by 10, if they prefer to prepare a larger quantity of product in a 30 quart bowl. This calculation will yield the number of ounces the baker must scale of each ingredient. A dough hook must be used with these types of mixing bowls to properly develop the gluten structure in the dough.

If the conversion from grams to ounces is done properly, 1000 g flour becomes 50 oz. (3 lb., 2 oz.) flour for the 20 quart bowl or 100 oz. (6 lb., 4 oz.) flour when a 30 quart bowl is used. Using the same procedure, 60 g sugar converts to 3 oz. and 6 oz. sugar respectively.

References

Carlin, G. 1958. The Fundamental Chemistry of Bread Making. American Society of Bakery Engineers, Proceedings.

Anonymous. 1993. How to Evaluate a Cream Yeast System. Gist-brocades, Baking Update.

Anonymous. 1993. Deciding Between Fresh Yeast and Dry Yeast. Gist-brocades, Baking Update.

Vetter, J.L. Ph.D., 1993. *Food Labeling*, American Institute of Baking, V-15.

Fagrell, E., *Raisin Usage in Baked Goods*. 1992. Technical Bulletin, American Institute of Baking. XIV(4)

Formula 1
White Pan Bread
(No-Time Straight Dough)

Baker's Percent	Weight Grams	Ingredients
100	1000	Bread Flour (11.5% Protein)
6	60	Granulated Sugar
4	40	Nonfat Dry Milk
2	20	Salt
0.5	5	Mineral Yeast Food
0.006	(60 ppm)	Ascorbic Acid
3	30	Bread Shortening
3.5	35	Compressed Yeast
64	640	Water (Variable)
183.006	**1830**	**Total Amount**

Mix:	To full gluten development.
Dough Temperature:	82°F (28°C).
Floor Time:	10 minutes.
Scaling Weight:	18.5 oz. (525 g) per 1 lb. (454 g) loaf.
Proof:	About 60 minutes at 109°F (43°C) to full proof.
Bake:	16-18 minutes at 450°F (232°C).
Cool :	One hour under ambient conditions on cooling rack.

Formula 2
White Pan Bread
(Fermented Straight Dough)

Baker's Percent	Weight Grams	Ingredients
100	1000	Bread Flour (11.5% Protein)
6	60	Granulated Sugar
2	20	Nonfat Dry Milk
2	20	Salt
0.5	5	Mineral Yeast Food
3	30	Bread Shortening
3	30	Compressed Yeast
62	620	Water (Variable)
178.5	**1785**	**Total Amount**

Mix: To full gluten development.
Dough Temperature: 78-80°F (25.5-26.5°C).
Floor Time: 1 - 1.5 hours at 84°F (29°C).
Scaling Weight: 18.5 oz. (525 g) per 1 lb. (454 g) loaf.
Proof: About 60 minutes at 109°F (43°C) to full proof.
Bake: 16-18 minutes at 450°F (232°C)
Cool: One hour under ambient conditions on cooling rack.

Formula 3
White Pan Bread
(Sponge and Dough Method)

Baker's Percent	Weight Grams	Ingredients
Sponge: (Preferment)		
70	700	Bread Flour (11.5% Protein)
0.5	5	Mineral Yeast Food
2.5	25	Compressed Yeast
42	420	Water
Dough: (Remix)		
30	300	Bread Flour (11.5% Protein)
9	90	42% High-Fructose Corn Syrup
2	20	Nonfat Milk Solids
2	20	Salt
3	30	Bread Shortening
15	150	Water and Ice (Variable)
176	1760	Total Amount

Sponge: *Temperature:* 74-77°F (24-25°C).
Fermentation Time: 3.5 to 4 hours at 84°F (29°C).

Dough: *Mix:* To full gluten development
Temperature: 78-80°F (25.5-26.5°C).
Floor Time: 10-15 min. under ambient conditions.

Scaling Weight: 18.5 oz. (525 g) per 1 lb. (454 g) loaf.

Proof: About 60 minutes at 109°F (43°C) to full proof.

Bake: 16-18 minutes at 450°F (232°C)

Cool: One hour under ambient conditions on rack or conveyor

Formula 4
White Pan Bread
(40% Flour Liquid Sponge and Dough Method)

Baker's Percent	Weight Grams	Ingredients
		Liquid Sponge: (Preferment)
40	400	Bread Flour (11.5% Protein)
0.5	5	Salt
0.5	5	Mineral Yeast Food
0.006	(60 ppm)	Ascorbic Acid
3	30	Compressed Yeast
50	500	Water
		Dough: (Remix)
60	600	Bread Flour (11.5% Protein)
8.5	85	42% High-Fructose Corn Syrup
2	20	Nonfat Dry Milk
1.5	15	Salt
2	20	Vegetable Oil
1	10	Crumb Softener (Hydrated)
7.5	75	Water and Ice (Variable)
176.506	**1765**	**Total Amount**

Liquid Sponge: *Initial Temperature:* 80°F (27°C).
Fermentation Time: 2 hours at 84°F (29°C).
Holding Temperature: 41°F (5°C).

Note: A liquid sponge prepared for a single dough may be used right after the fermentation is complete and without cooling to the recommended holding temperature. Liquid ferments used for more than one dough must be chilled to and stored at the recommended holding temperature until they are needed for dough mixing.

Dough: *Mix:* To full gluten development.
Temperature: 78 - 80°F (25.5-26.5°C).
Floor Time: 15 minutes.
Scaling Weight: 18.5 oz. (525 g) dough per 1 lb. loaf.
Proof: About 55 minutes at 109°F (43°C) to full proof.
Bake: 16 to 18 minutes at 450°F (232°C).
Cool: One hour under ambient conditions on cooling rack.

Formula 5
White Pan Bread
(No-Flour Water Brew and Dough Method)

Baker's Percent	Weight Grams	Ingredients
	Water Brew Ferment:	
3	30	42% High-Fructose Corn Syrup
0.5	5	Salt
0.2	2	Fermentation Buffer*
3	30	Compressed Yeast
43.5	435	Water
	Dough: (Remix)	
100	1000	Bread Flour (11.5% Protein)
10	100	42% High-Fructose Corn Syrup
2	20	Milk Replacer
1.5	15	Salt
0.06	0.6	Ammonium Sulfate
0.25	2.5	Monocalcium Phosphate
0.5	5	Sodium Stearoyl Lactylate
3	30	Bread Shortening
0.009	(90 ppm)	Ascorbic Acid
16.8	168	Water and Ice (Variable)
184.319	**1843.1**	**Total Amount**

*Fermentation Buffer: Ingredient Legend: Calcium carbonate, ammonium sulfate, flour, salt and calcium sulfate.

Water Brew Ferment: *Initial Temperature:* 80°F (27°C).
Fermentation Time: 1 hr at 84°F (29°C).
Holding Temperature: 41°F (5°C).

Note: By cooling the brew ferment to 41°F (5°C), the yeast becomes inactive and the ferment may be held in this state for several hours. The cold brew also makes it easier to control the dough temperature at the remix stage.

Dough: *Mix:* To full gluten development.
    Temperature: 78-80°F (25.5-26.5°C).

Floor Time: 15 minutes at ambient temperature.
Scaling Weight: 18.5 oz. (525 g) dough per 1 lb. (454 g) loaf.
Proof: About 55 minutes at 109°F (43°C) to full proof.
Bake: 16 to 18 minutes at 450°F (232°C).
Cool: One hour under ambient conditions on rack or conveyor.

Formula 6
Hamburger Buns
(Straight Dough Method)

Baker's Percent	Weight Grams	Ingredients
100	1000	Bread Flour (11.7% Protein)
12	120	Granulated Sugar
2	20	Salt
0.5	5	Mineral Yeast Food
0.009	(90 ppm)	Ascorbic Acid
0.0045	(45 ppm)	Azodicarbonamide (ADA)
6	60	Bread Shortening
3	30	Compressed Yeast
64	640	Water and Ice (variable)
187.5135	**1875**	**Total Amount**

Dough:	*Mix:* To full gluten development.
	Temperature: 78 ± 1°F (25.5 ± 0.5°C).
	Fermentation Time: One hour at 84°F (29°C).
Scaling Weight:	2 oz.. (56 g) dough per unit.
Make-up:	Round dough pieces tightly with palm of hand.
Intermediate Proof:	5 minutes under ambient conditions.
Sheeting:	Flatten dough pieces by passing them through a moulder/sheeter with a 3/8 inch (9.5 millimeter) gap.
Pan:	Silicone-glazed bun pan with 3.5 inch diameter cups or on aluminum sheet pan lined with treated paper.
Proof:	To 40 millimeter (1.575 inch) template (full proof): approximately 55 to 60 minutes at 109°F (43°C).
Bake:	9-10 minutes at 435°F (224°C).
Cool:	30 minutes under ambient conditions on cooling rack

Formula 7
Hamburger Buns
(Sponge and Dough Method)

Baker's Percent	Weight Grams	Ingredients
	Sponge: (Preferment)	
80	800	Bread Flour (12.5% Protein)
0.5	5	Mineral Yeast Food
3	30	Compressed Yeast
46	460	Water
	Dough: (Remix)	
20	200	Bread Flour (12.5% Protein)
17	170	42% High Fructose Corn Syrup
2	20	Salt
0.003	(30 ppm)	Ascorbic Acid
0.001	(10 ppm)	Azodicarbonamide (ADA)
6	60	Bread Shortening
10	100	Water and Ice (variable)
174.504	**1745**	**Total Amount**

Sponge:	*Temperature:* 74-77°F (24-25°C).
	Fermentation Time: 3.5-4 hours at 84°F (29°C).
Dough:	*Mix:* To full gluten development.
	Temperature: 78-80°F (25.5-26.5°C).
Floor Time:	5-10 min. under ambient conditions.
Scaling Weight:	2 oz. (56 g) dough per unit.
Make-up:	Round dough pieces tightly with palm of hand.
Intermediate Proof:	5 minutes under ambient conditions.
Sheeting:	Flatten dough pieces by passing them through a moulder/sheeter with a 3/8 inch (9.5 millimeter) gap.
Pan:	Silicone-glazed bun pan with 3.5 inch diameter cups or on aluminum sheet pan lined with treated paper liner.
Proof:	To 40 millimeter (1.575 inch) template (full proof).
	Approximately 55-60 minutes at 109°F (43°C).
Bake:	9-10 minutes at 435°F (224°C).
Cool:	30 minutes under ambient conditions on cooling rack.

Cake Baking

Test Baking

The axiom for experimental baking is: Take nothing for granted! Use experience to make new judgments and never depend on old judgments! Every formula, no matter how functional it was in the past, must be reoptimized before it is used for new research or for the evaluation of an ingredient. Ingredients, such as flour and shortening, change in performance from shipment to shipment and even under the best storage conditions. It is not unusual for a previously optimized cake formula to require an adjustment in the amount of water and emulsifier added to the batter.

Although all formulations presented in this book have been test-baked and checked for tolerance, they may still need to be modified slightly for optimum performance and to yield the desired information and quality characteristics. If these formulations are to be used to evaluate egg or milk products, it is best to slightly reduce the egg content to produce more tender cakes. Structural flaws caused by inferior ingredients are easier to recognize in cakes with a reduced resilience.

Cake Ingredients

The basic ingredients used for chemically leavened cakes are quite different from those used for bread production. Cakes are more tender and sweeter. Instead of being leavened (aerated) by carbon dioxide produced by yeast activity, cakes are leavened by a combination of air incorporated into the batter during mixing and by carbon dioxide released by a reaction of sodium bicarbonate (baking soda) with an acid or an acid salt. The proportions of ingredients used in cake systems also differ significantly from yeast-raised doughs.

Primary Cake Ingredients

The primary ingredients used in cake batters are flour, sugar, water, fat, and eggs. Although most cakes are prepared with chemical leavening (baking powder), this ingredient is not necessary when sufficient fat and egg levels are used. The sugar level in cake batters is usually very high and often exceeds the amount of flour in the formula. The amount of water added to the batter is critical and depends on the sugar level. Although eggs aid in the aeration of the batter, their primary purpose in most cakes is to provide additional structure to the cake crumb. Since vegetable oils are unable to retain air in a batter system, plastic fats, such as shortening, margarine, and butter, are usually used in cake systems.

Cake Flour

Cake flour is milled from soft winter wheat grown primarily east of the Mississippi River. Although some cake flour is milled from white wheat and from hard red winter wheat, the great majority of it is produced from soft red winter wheat. What distinguishes cake flour from cookie and ordinary pastry flour is its treatment with chlorine gas. Chlorination modifies the flour protein, the lipids, and the starch components through oxidation. The amount of chlorine added to flour ranges from 0.11-0.23% (about 2-4 oz. per 100 lbs. flour) and can be determined by the pH of the flour. The optimum pH for most cake flours is 4.8±0.1. Higher values may limit the amount of sugar that can be added to the batter and lower values may require reformulation, such as higher levels of emulsifier.

Cake flour is available in different qualities. Most cake flour now used by larger bakeries in snack cake production is a *long patent flour* with a 90-95% separation rate (See previous chapter under *Milling of Flour*). This flour has a protein range of 7-9% and an ash content of 0.36-0.40%. Premium cake flour is usually a *short patent flour* (70-80% separation) with a protein content ranging from 7 -8.5% and an ash content of 0.33-0.37%. All these cake flours are chlorinated. Nonchlorinated wheat flours will not produce quality cakes with sugar levels greater than the amount of flour in the formula. The resulting cakes tend to have a collapsed crumb structure with a gummy mouthfeel, similar to the crumb structure found in "fudgy" brownies.

The cake flour milled from hard red winter wheat performs slightly differently from flour milled from soft wheat. It is produced by a special milling process known as *turbo milling*. This technology separates the flour by "air classification" into two fractions differing in the protein content. While the protein-rich fraction is blended into regular bread flour, the low-protein fraction is processed into cake flour by chlorine treatment (4.7-5.0 pH). The ash content of the turbo-milled cake flour ranges from 0.34-0.4. But the major difference between the turbo-milled hard wheat and soft wheat cake flours is their content of damaged starch. The 8-12% damaged starch content in the turbo-milled hard wheat cake flour produces batters with a higher viscosity than equivalent soft wheat flours with 2.5-3.5% starch damage.

Cake flours from hard turbo-milled wheat tends to produce slightly lower volumes in layer cakes and a tougher crumb structure. This may lead to a slight reduction in the egg level in the formula. Because the lipids in soft wheat flour are more exposed by the milling process than lipids in hard wheat flour, the turbo-milled hard wheat cake flour is the flour of choice for angel food cakes. In fact, it is the only flour suitable for angel food cake production using continuous mixers. Cake flour turbo-milled from soft wheat functions more like regular cake flour.

Sweeteners

Although layer cakes have been made with liquid sugar (67% sucrose and 33% water), best results are obtained with a fine granulated sugar. Alternate sugars, such as dextrose, invert sugar, lactose, and corn syrups will not produce high-quality cakes when used to replace more than 25% of the sucrose. The low solubility of dextrose at room temperature will cause it to crystallize within 24 hours after baking and to form a firm and very crumbly crumb structure and a crust full of white "sugar spots" (sugar bloom). Corn syrups interfere with batter aeration and tend to reduce the cake volume. High-fructose corn syrup (HFCS) has a similar effect and tends to cause Maillard, or browning, reactions not only in the crust, but also in the crumb. This reaction produces a darker crumb color and a bitter and unpleasant taste. Chocolate cakes made with HFCS also lack the reddish hue in the crumb color when 50% or more of the sugar is replaced with this syrup. The addition of extra baking soda to the chocolate cake batter will not alleviate this crumb color problem.

Shortening

Layer cakes are partially leavened by air incorporated into the batter during mixing. In sponge cakes the air is contained in the foam formed by egg protein. But most layer cakes are prepared with 10-60% (f.b.) cake shortening. The emulsifier in the cake shortening facilitates the incorporation of air into the batter. The emulsifier in regular cake shortening is usually a medium firm monoglyceride or a mixture of mono- and diglycerides. Shortenings used for cake mixes or fluid shortenings are generally formulated with a blend of propylene glycol monoesters (PGME) and monoglycerides. Lactylated monoglycerides are very functional,too, but are rarely used anymore. The addition of lecithin makes these shortenings more functional in white layer cakes.

The quality of cake shortenings depends not only on their emulsifier system, but also on the source of the fat, the processing conditions used, and how the finished product was tempered. Shortenings function best in cake batters when their crystals are in the *beta-prime* form. While fats high in palm oil tend to crystallize naturally in this form, fats low in *palmitic acid*, a fatty acid with 16 carbon atoms, form the more stable, but less desirable *beta crystals*. Shortenings manufactured from partially hydrogenated soybean oil, which contains less than 11% palmitic acid, must be votated (quickly chilled with a high-efficiency heat exchanger) under very controlled conditions followed by tempering at 82-84°F (28-29°C) for a minimum of two days. Subsequent exposure to temperatures higher than the tempering temperature is harmful to the shortening's ability to cream properly and should be avoided. Shortenings may, however, be stored for up to one year under refrigeration.

Good quality layer cakes may be prepared with shortening levels as high as 50-60% (f.b.). At these levels, a sufficient amount of monoglyceride is added with the high-ratio cake shortening to produce layer cakes of optimum quality. As the shortening level is reduced to less than 50% of the flour weight, additional emulsifier must be added to the batter.

The type of cake emulsifier used most commonly for this purpose is a blend of monoglycerides, polysorbate 60, sorbitan monostearate, and propylene glycol monoesters. For greatest effectiveness, these emulsifiers are used in the hydrated form. As less and less shortening is used in the formulation, the amount of cake emulsifier is increased. Excessive levels of this type of cake emulsifier will cause a collapse of the crumb structure near the bottom of the layer cakes.

High shortening levels tend to depress the volume of layer cakes. Sponge cakes made with about 6% hydrated cake emulsifier but without shortening will produce the largest cake volume. Shortening has, however, a beneficial effect on the shelf-life of cakes.

Eggs

The exact composition of fresh whole eggs varies with the size of the eggs, but the proportion of egg white in liquid whole eggs is in the range of 65-70%. The remainder is egg yolk which contains all the fat and cholesterol. The solids content in the various liquid or frozen egg components varies from about 11.5% in egg whites (egg albumen) and 24.5% in whole eggs, to 43% in egg yolk. The trend, however, is, for the solids content in whole eggs to increase to above 25%. This is caused by the increased demand for egg albumen and the decreased demand for egg yolk. This has given many commercial egg processors the incentive to add extra yolk to whole eggs. In most cases, such "fortifying" of whole eggs has only a beneficial effect on the baked product in which the egg is used.

Although not totally accurate, most bakers use the following conversion table for calculating the amount of dry egg and water they need to replace the equivalent liquid components.

Conversion Table

100% Liquid Whole Eggs = 25% Dry Whole Eggs + 75% Water
100% Liquid Egg Whites = 12.5% Egg Albumen + 87.5% Water
100% Liquid Egg Yolk   = 45% Dry Yolk + 55% Water

In most cases, the discrepancies in this conversion table will not affect product quality.

The amount of whole eggs added to batters depends on the end use of the cake. A sponge cake used for jelly rolls must contain a higher level of eggs than a sponge layer cake. Cakes baked and used as single layers do not need to have the same resilience, i.e., crumb strength, as cakes subjected to more handling, such as two-layer decorated cakes. Eggs are "tougheners" and structure-forming ingredients and their use-level in the liquid form must equal or exceed that of shortening in the cake. Despite popular belief, high levels of whole eggs and egg whites in baked food will not assure a moist mouthfeel when the product is consumed.

With today's available technologies, there should be no difference in the functionality of various types of eggs, whether they are fresh (refrigerated), frozen, or spray-dried. Individual bakeries generally develop a preference for one type of egg or another. Quite often this decision is influenced by disposal problems with the shipping containers. By federal mandate, all commercially produced eggs must be pasteurized and inspected by the United States Department of Agriculture (USDA). They must also test negative for Salmonella bacteria.

Frozen eggs were the choice of most bakers until the disposal of metal containers became a problem. Refrigerated eggs in self-contained refrigerated mobile tanks then grew in popularity. But fresh eggs are subject to fluctuations in price, and many bakers switched to dry eggs, which they are able to contract for far in advance. However, the purchaser of dried egg products must be aware of differences in egg quality due to drying conditions used during processing.

Room temperature stable (RTS) liquid whole eggs containing 50% sugar and only one third of the normal moisture (25%) are now successfully used by a growing number of bakers who are not afraid of making the proper adjustments in the amounts of sugar and water added to their batters. A baker who replaces fresh whole eggs with RTS eggs must use the same amount. But at the same time, the sugar in the formula must be reduced by half of the weight of RTS eggs and the amount of water added to the batter must be increased by the same quantity.

Egg whites often contain a *whipping agent*. The whipping agent has no adverse effect in products not requiring "whipping" (aeration) of the albumen. Whipping agents most commonly used are *sodium lauryl sulfate* and *triethyl citrate*. They can be added to either liquid egg whites or to dry egg albumen.

The main function of whole eggs and egg whites in layer cakes is to provide structure. Egg protein gives the cake crumb resiliency and sufficient toughness for handling after baking. Layer cakes formulated with an insufficient amount of eggs are very fragile and tend to break apart during processing. In most batters formulated with a significant amount of shortening, the ability of eggs to aerate and emulsify is of lesser importance.

Egg coloring is usually a blend of the certified food colors Yellow #5 and Yellow #6. Beta carotene may also be used.

Chemical Leavening

Chemical leavening is the result of a reaction between *sodium bicarbonate* and one or more leavening acids. This reaction releases carbon dioxide gas that enlarges the tiny air cells created during the mixing process. Although air incorporated into the batter during mixing contributes to the leavening of cakes in the oven, much of the leavening action in layer cakes comes from the chemical leavening agents added to the batter. The incorporated air provides for most of the *nucleation*, i.e., the formation of a multitude of small gas cells able to absorb additional leavening gas released by chemical leaveners during baking.

The following table shows the most commonly used leavening acids and acid salts with their neutralizing value and their reaction rate:

Leavening Acid/Salt	Neutralizing Value	Reaction Rate
Sodium Aluminum Phosphate	100	Slow
Sodium Acid Pyrophosphate 22	72	Slow
Sodium Acid Pyrophosphate 28	72	Medium
Sodium Aluminum Sulfate	103	Medium
Glucono-delta-lactone	45	Medium (Constant)
Sodium Acid Pyrophosphate 40	72	Fast
Anhydrous Monocalc. Phosphate	83	Delayed, very fast
Monocalc. Phosphate Monohydrate	80	Very fast
Cream of Tartar	45	Very fast

The *neutralizing value* is defined as the parts by weight of sodium bicarbonate (baking soda) required to neutralize 100 parts by weight of the respective leavening acid or salt. Thus, 72 grams of baking soda will neutralize 100 grams of *sodium acid pyrophosphate 28* (SAPP 28), a major component of many commercial baking powders and *acid creams*. Acid creams are used as a substitute for *cream of tartar* (potassium acid tartrate) to acidify batters and doughs, i.e., to lower their pH slightly.

Baking powder is composed of 30% sodium bicarbonate and a sufficient quantity of one or more leavening acid salts to neutralize the baking soda. Besides SAPP 28, *sodium aluminum phosphate* (SALP) and *sodium aluminum sulfate* (SAS) are also used as leavening agents.

Many types of baking powder contain about 5% monocalcium phosphate monohydrate which releases approximately 13.3% of the available carbon dioxide in a *double-acting baking powder* while the batter is being mixed.

This early released leavening gas aids the incorporated air in the nucleation process. A well nucleated batter tends to give the baked cake a finer and more uniform cell structure. Since emulsified cake shortenings facilitate batter aeration, cakes formulated with a higher shortening level generally provide a better basis for nucleation than low fat cakes.

Salt

In chemically and air-leavened high-sugar products, salt helps to modify the sweetness of the product and improves their taste. Some baked goods also tend to form severe sugar bloom (white spots formed by crystallized sugar in the crust) when salt is inadvertently left out of the formula. The salt level is usually adjusted to 2-4% (f.b.).

Leaner formulas are on the lower end of this range and rich formulations approach the upper limit.

For types of salt available to the baking industry, refer to pages 77-81 of this volume.

Water

Water is one of the most important ingredients in every bakery food. It is added to doughs and batters either directly, or as part of milk (88%), whole eggs (75%), egg whites (88%) and/or corn syrup (20-29%). The addition level and the rate of addition are very critical in cake batters. It affects not only the cake volume, appearance, and eating quality, but also the symmetry and crumb structure of the layer cakes. While excessive amounts of water in the batter will depress the cake volume and cause a "peaked" cake contour, a shortage in liquids can cause the cake center to collapse and have a depression in the center. Cakes with a good general crumb structure but an open grain at the top center require more water (10-20% f.b.) in the formula.

Secondary Cake Ingredients

The secondary cake ingredients give cakes their special characteristics. They are too numerous to mention all of them. This ingredient group includes milk solids and replacers, cocoa and chocolate, flavors, fruits, gums, and starches.

Milk and Milk Replacers

Traditionally, nonfat dry milk (NFDM) has been used in layer cakes at the 10% (f.b.) level. However, rising milk prices forced many bakers to search for other ingredients to replace the milk solids. At the 10% level NFDM toughens the cake crumb and gives it resilience for improved handling characteristics. This effect is achieved by the casein portion of the milk protein and the calcium ions present in milk. Although most bakers use milk solids subjected to high-heat treatment, this treatment is not necessary for high-sugar layer cakes. Untreated milk has an adverse effect on the gluten structure in yeast-leavened bakery foods, but not in chemically leavened products.

Even though many different milk replacers are offered to the baking industry, only those formulated with caseinate have been found to be as functional as NFDM in layer cakes. Bakers using replacers based on soy protein isolates and whey protein concentrates often find it necessary to reformulate their cakes. Many bakers have simply reduced the amount of NFDM in their cakes, often to as low as 5%, to compensate for the increased cost of this ingredient. Most functional milk replacers for cakes utilize whey. But, if used by itself in place of NFDM, whey will produce very tender and fragile layer cakes.

Some milk replacers producing poor quality layer cakes may still produce snack cakes of good quality. The relatively small size of snack cakes makes them less subject to breakage, especially when they receive a good bake from the bottom to form a strong sidewall.

Cocoa and Chocolate

The distinction between devil's food and chocolate cakes no longer exists. Cakes made with cocoa as the only source of chocolate flavor can now be called *chocolate cake* just like cakes prepared with chocolate liquor. Because of the difficulty of melting chocolate without overheating for incorporation into the batter, most bakers are now using cocoa powder in their cakes. The public now accepts *devil's food cakes* made with cocoa as chocolate cakes. In fact, the term "devil's food cake" is slowly disappearing.

Cocoa powder is available as the slightly acidic *natural cocoa* (pH 5.2-5.8) and as *dutched cocoa* (pH more than 6.5). Each type of cocoa is also available with three different ranges of cocoa butter fat. *Breakfast cocoa* contains 22-24% cocoa butter and is used primarily in soft pie fillings and in beverages. Many small bakeries still use cocoa with 15-17% cocoa butter fat, but most bakeries today use cocoa with 10-12% cocoa butter fat. Low fat cocoas with less than 1% cocoa butter fat are now also available.

The "dutching process" was invented by Van Houten in the early 1800s. It raises the pH and darkens the color of the cocoa. It also changes the flavor slightly. Good quality cakes can be produced with either dutched cocoa or with untreated "natural cocoa." Since natural cocoa tends to be slightly cheaper than dutched cocoa, most large bakeries prefer to use the untreated type.

The color pigments in cocoa are very sensitive to changes in the acidity of the product. The higher the pH of chocolate cakes, the darker and more reddish brown the crumb color becomes. When the pH of the crumb is less than 7, the crumb assumes a grayish-brown color with very little red in it. For this reason, chocolate cakes are formulated with an excess of baking soda that raises the crumb pH to above 8.

Although retail bakers usually add 20-25% (f.b.) of 15-17% butter fat cocoa to their batters, large baking companies tend to use only 15-18% (f.b.), and sometimes even as little as 12% (f.b.), of a 10-12% butter fat cocoa in their product. Very high levels of baking soda (up to 4.5% f.b.) in cakes made with relatively low amounts of cocoa help to darken their crumb color.

Flavors

Flavor ingredients are used either to enhance the flavor of other cake ingredients or to give cakes a different and unique taste. Some of the ingredients, like egg yolk and cocoa, contribute their own taste and aroma. Other additives, like many fruits and vegetables, have insufficient flavor intensity to characterize the baked product and require the addition of a complementing aromatic essence. The baker may also choose to artificially flavor and color some products without using any naturally characterizing ingredient. Whenever flavors are used, artificially made or from other natural sources, the product label must indicate that a flavor has been added.

Manufacturers of flavorings use one or more solvents. Most of the flavors contain at least some water. Alcohol (ethanol) is used for extracts, while propylene glycol is used to emulsify and disperse many flavoring ingredients. Stable vegetable oils serve as solvents for some fat soluble flavor ingredients. Although extracts find much use in the ice cream industry, the alcohol tends to evaporate when exposed to air. The extracted aromatic components then often escape the product. Flavors using water, vegetable oil, and/or propylene glycol as solvents tend to be more stable in baked foods and are, therefore, more widely used by bakers.

Vanilla

Most cake formulations include some flavor to improve their eating quality. *Vanilla* is probably the most commonly used flavoring in cakes. There are three different vanilla categories:

Pure vanilla extract
Vanilla-vanillin
Imitation vanilla

The *pure vanilla extract* contains 35% or more alcohol. A "one-fold vanilla extract" is defined by the FDA as the product of 13.35 oz. vanilla beans per gallon flavoring. A "four-fold pure vanilla" requires 53.4 oz. vanilla beans per gallon. The three-fold and four-fold pure vanillas also contain more than 35% alcohol.

The *vanillin* is an artificial product made from lignin, a by-product of the paper industry. The refined product is known as "USP Lignin Vanillin" or plain *USP Vanillin*. The *Vanilla-Vanillin* is a specific blend of pure vanilla and one ounce of USP vanillin added per fold of vanilla. Thus, a four-fold pure vanilla has four ounces of vanillin added to it. *Ethyl vanillin* is three times as strong as regular vanillin and it cannot be substituted for USP vanillin in vanilla-vanillin. Ethyl vanillin is made from a coal tar derivative. Both vanillins give a clear solution when dissolved in water.

The flavor most commonly used by the baking industry is *imitation vanilla*. The basic component of this flavor is USP Vanillin and/or ethyl vanillin. "Artificial and natural vanilla" is the result of adding some natural component of vanilla beans to imitation vanilla. Many of these flavorings also contain a small amount of caramel color.

Imitation and "artificial and natural vanilla" flavorings come in many different concentrations, ranging up to the equivalent of a 24-fold vanilla. Therefore, the baker must be careful when comparing one type or brand of vanilla flavoring with another. Also, when purchasing large quantities of highly concentrated vanillin, the vanillin crystals may precipitate, especially during the cold season.

Although many formulations for bakery foods specify the amount of vanilla to be used, they rarely indicate the type or strength (fold) of the flavoring to be used. In fact, most bakers do not even know the strength of the vanilla they use in their own shop. Most vanillas fall into the range of 2-6 fold, but 24-fold imitation vanillas are not uncommon.

Imitation vanilla is also available in a dry form. Dextrins are usually used as carrier for the vanillin, which is often a blend of USP vanillin and ethyl vanillin.

Blends of vanilla with other flavorings are very popular. Butter-lemon flavor is popular and the combination of butter-lemon-vanilla (BLV) is an excellent flavoring for white layer cakes, snack cakes, and creme fillings.

Citrus Flavors

Like vanilla, citrus flavors are often found in cakes, cake donuts, icings, and fillings. Although lemon emulsions are used by many bakers, lemon powder and crystals are also used as primary flavoring ingredients.

Orange flavor is often found in combination with lemon flavor, particularly in cake donuts. This flavor combination has replaced spices in many donut formulations.

Butter Flavors

The unique flavor of butter is comprised of more than 120 flavor components falling into four different categories: fatty acids, lactones, methyl ketones, and dimethyl sulfide.

Although butter oil contains less than 10% of *short-chain fatty acids* (SCFA with 10 or less carbons in the acid chain), these fatty acids play an important role in the flavor profile. The flavor intensity of SCFAs is accentuated when the fat is hydrolyzed to form glycerin and free fatty acids.

A very small amount of free *lactones* is found in the fat phase of butter. Heating causes the formation of additional lactones from precursors and increases the butter's flavor intensity. Lactones contribute an essential component to the butter flavor of bakery products and confections. They are also an important part of butterscotch flavor.

Methyl ketones are formed from precursors when the butter is heated. Diacetyl is a major member of this group. Diacetyl is also produced in cultured butter by the bacterium *Streptococcus diacetilactis*. Diacetyl is the flavor component most frequently associated with a "strong" butter flavor.

Dimethyl sulfide is another important contributor to a pleasant butter flavor. It is present in butter at a perceptible level and helps to "smooth" the harsher flavor notes of diacetyl (Butter Facts 1991).

Butter flavors, dry or liquid, utilize members of one or more of these flavor components. Many of them are produced from cultured butter with or without hydrolysis of the butter fat. Depending on their composition and application, many butter flavors may or may not give satisfactory results in bakery foods.

Fruits and Vegetables

Fruits and vegetables are usually used to characterize a cake product. Whenever they are used, the baker must remember that these products contain between 85-95% moisture which must be compensated for in the formula balance.

Carrots and pumpkin are probably the most popular vegetable varieties used in cake products. To overcome the relatively bland taste of these two vegetables, bakers like to add spices to pumpkin and pineapple and raisins to carrots. They also must add relatively large amounts (60-100% f.b.) of these vegetables to their batters. Zucchinis and various types of squash are good alternatives for pumpkin.

Applesauce, bananas, strawberries, and blueberries are

good fruits to add directly to cake batters. The bland taste of applesauce is often enhanced with a little cinnamon and/ or nutmeg. The missing seeds in strained banana puree can be replaced with pecan meal which also tends to improve the flavor of the finished product.

In the past, raisins were often added to pound cakes and fruit cakes. However, few raisins are now used in chemically leavened bakery foods, although the popularity of yeast-raised raisin products has grown during the past three decades. The use of raisins in cake products seems to be limited to muffins and dark fruit cakes. There is no standard of identity for the use of raisins in cakes.

Gums

Gums are used in cakes primarily to control batter viscosity. Gums affect the batter flow before and during baking and are necessary in batters mixed in a single stage, as many cake mixes are. Without the addition of extra water, gums significantly increase batter viscosity. But they have practically no effect on the water activity of the baked product. The most commonly used gums are guar gum and xanthan gum; but locust bean gum, cellulose gums, and others also find applications in batter systems.

Starches and Maltodextrins

In the quest to produce cakes with a moist crumb and a long shelf-life, bakers started to add pregelatinized corn or tapioca starch to their batters along with extra water. Tapioca starch is often preferred because of the creamy texture it produces in the cake crumb. Pregelatinized starch is usually added at levels up to 5% of the flour weight. However, when too much water and starch is added, cakes may show severe shrinkage during cooling.

Maltodextrins are hydrolized starch from various

sources with a **Dextrose Equivalence** (DE) of less than 5. Their manufacturers generally claim that one part of maltodextrin with three parts of water can replace four parts of fat in bakery foods. This would result in a significant reduction in calories. Due to the inherent differences in the native (original) starches, the various maltodextrins affect the finished product texture slightly differently.

In general, hydrated maltodextrins produce a moist and pudding-like cake texture when used to replace more than half of the fat normally added to batters. The texture of cakes with all fat replaced with maltodextrins is often "gummy" and the crumb tends to give an undesirable mouthfeel. At higher usage levels of maltodextrins, cakes frequently lack volume and lose eye appeal. In most cake formulations, however, up to 25% of the total fat can easily be replaced with hydrated maltodextrins without a significant adverse effect on product quality. At higher replacement levels, the formulator must expect significant deviations from the original product quality.

High-Ratio Cakes

High-ratio layer cakes were introduced to the North American market during the decade prior to World War II. These cakes were a consequence of new ingredient technologies: chlorinated cake flour and emulsified shortening.

The term "high-ratio" signifies that the cake formula contains more sugar than flour. The amount of sugar in the batter affects the pasting (transformation of liquid batter into cake crumb) of the batter at the end of the baking stage. Sugar raises the pasting temperature which, for a long time, prevented bakers from adding more sugar than flour to their cake batters. Higher sugar levels prevented the starch in the flour from gelatinizing during pasting and caused the cakes to collapse. Bakers, however, use this property of starch in the presence of high sugar levels to produce *fudgy brownies*. But "fudgy" cakes are usually not desired.

As bakeries grew in size, and corner grocery stores became supermarkets, large wholesale bakers needed cakes with a longer shelf-life. A higher sugar level in the cakes seemed to be the answer to this problem. Research had shown that treating the flour with chlorine not only whitened (bleached) the flour, but also lowered the pasting temperature of the batter sufficiently to offset the adverse effect of the high sugar level. Adding more water to the batter also seemed to be beneficial, and this was made possible by the addition of monoglycerides to the shortening. Thus, cake flour treated with chlorine to lower its pH to about 4.8 became known as *high-ratio flour* and the emulsified shortening was called *high-ratio cake shortening*.

The first high-ratio layer cakes had a shortening level of about 50-60% of the flour weight. The amount of sugar generally varied from 100-140%, but averaged around 120% (f.b.). The water level, including the moisture in liquid eggs, milk, and syrups, always exceeded the amount of sugar in the formula. This excess could be as little as 10% (f.b.) for sugar levels of 110-120%, or as much as 20-30% (f.b.) more water than sugar in cakes formulated with 140% or more sugar. However, since the shortages of sugar and shortening during the early 1970s, there has been a noticeable trend to lower sugar and fat levels in commercial layer cakes.

Batter Emulsification

The reduction in emulsified cake shortening levels also resulted in less emulsifier being added to the batter. The total amount of sugar and liquid in the formula, however, remained the same. This made it necessary to add a small amount of cake emulsifier to batters with less than 50% emulsified shortening. The cake emulsifier is usually a hydrated blend of polysorbate 60, sorbitan monostearate, and monoglycerides. Propylene glycol esters of fatty acids are frequently also part of such an emulsifier blend. These emulsifier systems not only provide for emulsification, but they also facilitate the aeration of batters during mixing.

Nucleation of Batter

Although air incorporated into the batter during mixing contributes to the leavening of cakes in the oven, most of the leavening action in cake products comes from the chemical leavening agents added to the batter. The incorporated air provides for most of the *nucleation*, i.e., the formation of a multitude of small gas cells able to absorb additional leavening gas released by chemical leaveners during baking. Many types of baking powder contain about 5% anhydrous monocalcium phosphate which releases approximately 13.3% of the available carbon dioxide in a double-acting baking powder while the batter is being mixed. The portion of gas that is released early by the chemical leavening ingredients aids the incorporated air in the nucleation process. A well nucleated batter tends to give the baked cake a finer and more uniform cell structure. Also, batters formulated with a higher shortening level generally provide a better basis for nucleation than low fat cakes.

Batter Temperature

It is very important to control the temperature of the ingredients and batter during mixing. For reliable experimental work, the ingredients must be kept in an air-conditioned room and the ambient temperature in the mixing area must be kept constant.

The functionality of emulsifiers used by the baking industry changes with temperature. Practically all food emulsifiers and emulsifier systems, including cake emulsifiers, were developed in air-conditioned baking laboratories kept at an arbitrary "average" temperature, i.e., they were inadvertently designed to perform best in the temperature range of 72-78°F (22-25.5°C). At higher temperatures, the emulsifiers tend to become more effective and the batters and creme icings appear to be overemulsified. The opposite is true at lower temperatures.

Temperature also affects the performance of most shortenings. As the temperature increases above the optimum range of 72-78°F (22-25.5°C), the shortening becomes increasingly softer, because more and more fat crystals melt and become liquid oil. As the solids in the shortening decrease in amount, the fat's capacity to hold water and air is impaired, the batters become less viscous and usually assume a very smooth appearance (over-emulsification). A slight increase in batter temperature can thus result in a significant increase in batter specific gravity (density of the mix relative to the density of water). However, when the temperature of the batter is less than about 72°F (22°C), more of the soft fraction in the fat solidifies (crystallizes) and causes the shortening to become too firm for incorporating air, i.e., creaming. The appearance of cold batters also tends to be more curdled (under-emulsified).

If air conditioning is not available, the effect on batter and icing temperature can be minimized by proper mixing procedures. When the temperature of ingredients and/or air is too low, higher mixing speeds tend to cause friction, and excess mixing energy is stored in the mix as heat. This method can raise the mix temperature by several degrees, thus enhancing the ability of the shortening to incorporate air into the mix.

Conversely, when the ambient air is too warm, high-speed mixing should be avoided. During high-speed mixing a large amount of ambient air is incorporated into the mix. While some of this air is absorbed, much of it merely displaces cooler air already incorporated into the batter or icing. This process raises the temperature of the ingredients in the batter. As the temperature of the batter or icing increases above the optimum temperature range for the fat, the shortening gradually loses its ability to hold air and the specific gravity increases. Therefore, the general rule for mixing batters and icings, even in large production, is to mix at high speed when the bakery is cold and at low speed when the bakery is warm. Once the temperature of the mix reaches about 84°F (29°C), most shortenings no longer have the ability to function as designed or intended.

Batter Mixing
Conventional Mixing

The most commonly used mixer in small bakeries and in baking laboratories is of a vertical configuration. The size of mixing bowls ranges from 5 quarts to 30 quarts (1 US quart = 0.95 liter). The 5 and 12 quart bowl sizes and corresponding flat "paddle beaters" (agitators) are generally preferred for mixing experimental cake batters. Bakers in small retail shops usually prefer larger bowl sizes for more mixing capacity. Other mixing attachments, like wire whips, are also available for most mixers and bowls. While the agitators turn, they orbit around the center of the bowls, thus providing for a very efficient, thorough mixing action.

There are many different mixing procedures used by the baking industry. Some of these originated at a time when chemical leavening agents were either not available or not suitable for the specific application. These methods are often complicated and for good results require a skilled person with good judgment.

Although some baking laboratories have continuous batter mixers available, most baking technologists use small vertical mixers and conventional mixing methods. The four-stage mixing method for batters is not only popular, but also very reliable for experimental baking. It can be used for most chemically leavened batters. The four stages of batter mixing with a vertical mixer comprise the following important procedures:

1. Blending of dry ingredients.
2. Mixing: Wetting of ingredients and elimination of lumps.
3. Creaming: Incorporation of air and nucleation.
4. Finishing: Subdividing and stabilizing of air cells.

All four mixing stages are important and contribute to product quality. The *blending* step disperses all the dry ingredients and prevents them from forming lumps when water is added. Blending is generally done for one minute at low speed to minimize loss of ingredients as dust. The shortening is best added and incorporated after the dry mix has been wetted with the first ingredient water. The baking technician must then make sure that all the shortening is properly incorporated into the mix and not stuck to the mixing attachment or mixing bowl.

During the *mixing* phase, the ingredients are hydrated and a stiff batter mass is formed. By mixing for 1 minute at low speed and for 3-5 minutes at medium speed on a 3-speed mixer, the mass becomes relatively homogeneous. The batter must be stiff enough so ingredient lumps are broken up and no significant amount of air is incorporated. Approximately 37-45% of the total formula water is normally required to produce this batter consistency.

In order to facilitate the incorporation of air, another 23-30% of the total water is added to the batter. After the addition of this liquid, the mixing bowl and agitator are thoroughly scraped with a rubber spatula. The water is then incorporated by mixing for 1 minute at low speed, followed by 2-3 minutes at medium speed. The length of this *creaming* phase is determined by the desired final specific gravity of the batter. At the end of the creaming stage, the specific gravity of the batter should be slightly less than the desired final specific gravity. The last addition of liquids will then raise the specific gravity to the desired level.

After the addition of the remaining water (28-33% of the total liquids), the mixing bowl and agitator should be scraped again to make sure that all ingredients are properly incorporated. From now on, the batter should be mixed only at slow speed. No additional air should be incorporated during the *finishing* stage, which rarely exceeds two minutes.

The purpose of this last and very important mixing phase is to disperse the incorporated air as very small gas bubbles. The gas released by the monocalcium phosphate in double acting baking powder combines with the air incorporated during the creaming phase and contributes to this important nucleation process. During the baking phase, these tiny air and gas cells are enlarged by the remaining leavening gas and form the cell structure for the cake crumb.

Continuous Mixing

Continuous batter mixers are available with 2 and 4 inch diameter mixing chambers (rotor heads). Only the 4 inch model has some very limited value for research and product development work, provided it is equipped with digital control gauges and used with chilled fluids or refrigerants circulating around the mixing chamber. However, the baking technologist must be aware of the fact that the mixing parameters for this laboratory mixer model differ even more significantly from the parameters used for 8 inch production mixers than the settings for an 8 inch mixer model differ from those for 10 and 14 inch models. The reason for this is the tangential velocity of the rotor, which is so much greater for larger diameter mixing heads. An eight inch diameter rotor moves twice as fast at the periphery (external boundary) as a 4 inch diameter rotor and it has over four times as much contact area for mixing. The same relationship exists between a 2 inch rotor and a 4 inch rotor, which makes it almost impossible to interpret the results obtained with such a small mixer for large-scale production.

Continuous batter mixers are only designed to homogenize and aerate batters. They do not proportion and blend ingredients. Therefore, the batter ingredients must be prescaled and blended in batches prior to "mixing" by the continuous mixer. These batches of unfinished batter are called *slurry*. Slurries must be uniform in specific gravity from batch to batch, or major adjustments in equipment settings become necessary whenever the slurry changes in density. Slurries should never be aerated to any significant extent, since aerated batter slurries are difficult to pump. This is because air compresses and expands with changes in pressure exerted by the pump. Batter slurries should also be kept cool to minimize the premature release of leavening gas.

Slurries can be prepared either with special high-speed slurry mixing equipment or with conventional horizontal or vertical batter mixers. Mixing is kept at a minimum and the incorporation of a significant amount of air is avoided. Batter slurries are usually mixed in two or three stages. During the first stage the ingredients are hydrated and ingredient lumps are prevented from forming. During the subsequent stages, the remaining liquids are added and incorporated to form a smooth slurry. High-speed slurry mixers use special high-shear agitators of various designs to prevent lumps from forming. Horizontal and high-speed slurry mixers usually have stationary mixing bowls and their fluid contents are pumped to a holding tank near the continuous mixer. To avoid clogging the valve below the tank, it is of utmost importance that a fluid ingredient, generally water, is always added first to a mixer with a stationary bowl.

The first adjustment made on a continuous mixer is the *pump* speed. The pump must deliver a specified amount of slurry volume to the mixer to meet the need of the batter depositor and to keep the oven fully loaded. Once the pump speed is properly adjusted, it should never be changed without good reason during the entire production run.

The next adjustment to be made is the *rotor* speed. The rotor "homogenizes" the batter by subdividing the incorporated air bubbles into very small gas cells. The rotor speed should be high enough to accomplish this task; but it should also be as low as possible to avoid unnecessary warming of the batter through friction heat. Because of differences in tangential velocity, the rotor speeds in large mixers are usually adjusted to lower revolutions per minute (RPM) than the speeds for smaller continuous mixers.

The *Air Flowrator* controls the amount of air injected into the batter. The injector for the air should always have a rubber tubing over the injector hole to prevent product from entering the Flowrator and the air supply line. The air line pressure must always be greater than the *back pressure* which controls the residence (dwell) time of the product in the mixing head. The back pressure is created and controlled either with a needle valve or with a pressurized rubber constriction at the exit from the mixing head. Different batters require different back pressures. Generally, the more air injected into batters, the greater the rotor speed and the back pressure must be.

The mixer operator must periodically check the specific gravity of the mixed batter, especially after a new slurry has been started, to make sure that there are no significant changes in the response of the batter to the mixing parameters. If the operator needs to make a major adjustment in any of the controls, changes in the other controls may also be necessary. The pump speed affects all other settings and the back pressure and rotor speed affect each other as well as the Flowrator setting.

Continuous mixers are not recommended for a limited production of cakes. Both the start-up and clean-up of the equipment are very time consuming. Since the ingredient slurries need to be scaled and mixed as batches every 20-30 minutes, little or no labor is saved in this operation. Continuous mixers are, however, ideally suited for automated cake production lines operating continuously.

Specific Gravity

In baking, the concept of *specific gravity* is used to measure the amount of air incorporated into a batter or a creme icing. Specific gravity is defined as the density of a product relative to the density of cold water. Unlike the concept of true density, which is expressed as pounds per cubic foot (lb./cu ft) or grams per cubic centimeter (g/cc), specific gravity has no units. A product lighter than water will have a specific gravity less than 1.0. A batter or product heavier than water has a specific gravity greater than 1.0

The specific gravity is calculated by dividing the weight of a specified volume of product, i.e., batter, by the weight of the same volume of water. A baker can do this by using a cup-like container with a level top, preferably made of stainless steel. Some bakeries use disposable paper cups with a 9 fluid ounce (266 cc) capacity with very good results.

After determining the weight of the cup (tare weight), the container is filled level with cold tap water and weighed to determine its gross weight. The net weight of the water is then the difference between the gross and tare weights. This procedure is repeated with batter and the net weight of the batter is then divided by the net weight of the water. Since aerated cake batters are usually lighter than water, their specific gravity is normally less than 1.0. Non-aerated batters and batters with a very high fruit content tend to have a specific gravity greater than 1.0.

The procedure for measuring the specific gravity is usually simplified by always using the same size measuring container (specific gravity cup) and by preparing a chart which translates gross batter weights into specific gravities.

Baking

Cakes are baked at lower temperatures than bread and buns. Batters need time for the leavening to be activated by the heat. If the batter "pastes" (is transformed from fluid batter to a rigid crumb) where it is in contact with the hot pan while still expanding significantly at the center, the product will "peak", i.e., the cake will be thicker at the center than at the outer edge. This undesirable cake characteristic is generally caused by too much heat in the oven. Most bakers prefer cakes with only a gentle "crown," i.e., a very slightly rounded top curvature, because level cakes are easier to "finish" with icing and to decorate.

Layer cakes are best baked at a temperature of 360±5°F (182±3°C) until their top center becomes firm and the cake starts to "pull away" from the pan, i.e., shrinks in size through moisture loss. If nonuniform heat conditions exist in the oven, e.g., when the oven is hotter on one side than on the other side, then the cake will not bake level. All fluid batters bake "away from the heat" — cakes will expand less on the side exposed to the higher temperature and tend to be higher in areas where they receive less heat.

When cakes are baked in multi-zone ovens with separate bottom and top heat controls, the first zone should provide heat (about 300-325°F or 149-163°C) only from the bottom to warm the batter and to activate the chemical leavening. There is usually enough heat carried over from the adjacent zone so that the top burner(s) in the first zone can be shut off. The bottom heat in the second of three baking zones should be slightly higher (about 340-360°F or 171-182°C) than in the first zone and the top heat should be adjusted to about 330-350°F (165-177°F). There may be a further increase in temperature for the third and last baking zone in which the baking process is completed.

Not all large ovens have three baking zones. Some have more zones and others may have only one zone, and each oven has its own baking profile and characteristics. All chemically leavened cakes should be allowed to expand uniformly before the pasting process begins at the sidewall of the pans. Convection and impingement ovens also tend to "bake hotter" than the same temperature in a regular gas fired reel or traveling tray oven. The suggested baking temperatures given here are, therefore, only to be considered as guides and to show the relationship between the different baking zones in an oven.

Cooling and Depanning

In commercial production, layer cakes are usually allowed to cool to room temperature before they are removed from the pan. This requires a very resilient crumb structure. In experimental and retail baking, however, layer cakes are often depanned five or ten minutes after baking. This is possible in experimental baking because the layer cake pans are usually lined on the bottom with a paper liner to facilitate the pan release. Also, the baking technician is able to handle the warm and very tender cakes more carefully than is possible in large automated bakeries.

The "rough" handling in automated bakeries "sets" the structure of the cakes by the jarring the cakes receive as they are mechanically unloaded from the oven. Cakes baked in baking laboratories with a high sugar to flour ratio often shrink severely during cooling. This can be avoided by dropping the cakes onto a hard surface from a height of approximately one or two inches when they are removed from the oven. This procedure accomplishes the same as the automated oven unloading equipment and it "sets" the cake structure immediately, preventing further shrinkage of the cake crumb during cooling. However, dense layer cakes, like white layer and high moisture cakes do not seem to benefit from this procedure.

Cake Evaluation

Determination of Specific Volume

After the cakes have cooled for about one hour under ambient conditions, they are weighed and measured for volume by rapeseed displacement. The specific cake volume is then calculated by dividing the volume in cubic centimeters (cc) by the weight in grams (g).

In the absence of a Volumeter (available from National Manufacturing Company in Lincoln, Nebraska), the volume of layer cakes can be measured by placing them into a larger pan and measuring the volume of rapeseed displaced by the cake in the pan.

In some cases, particularly when measuring the volume of white layer cakes, the rapeseed tends to adhere to the sticky cake crust. This phenomenon can be annoying and it may require frequent recalibration of the measuring device. The problem can be minimized or avoided entirely by covering the cake surface with a thin layer of granulated sugar or by carefully wrapping the cake in a very thin cling film. The error introduced by this method is small and can be compensated for by subtracting a nominal number of cubic centimeters from the total measured volume.

Scoring Cakes for Quality

As with bread, only the volume of cakes is based on an objective measurement. All other quality attributes are judged subjectively and can be grouped into three categories:

1. Appearance: Volume, Symmetry, Crust Color, Crust Character

2. Crumb Structure: Texture, Grain, Crumb Color
3. Sensory: Aroma, Taste, Mouthfeel

The volume score can be derived from an arbitrary table translating the specific volume into a volume score. The symmetry score indicates how closely the contour of the cake approaches the desired light "crown." Cakes with a "peak" at the center are difficult to stack and to ice. On the other hand, very flat cakes or cakes with a depression in the center indicate structural problems in the crumb. The crust color of the cakes should be uniform and "characteristic" for the cake variety. Crusts of cakes formulated with whole eggs should be relatively dry to the touch, while white cakes made with egg whites tend to be slightly tacky. This problem with a tacky crust becomes worse as more moisture from the internal crumb migrates to the cake surface during cooling.

The texture of cakes should be soft and moist with a good resilience to deformation, i.e., the crumb structure should recover immediately after it has been slightly compressed or "deformed." The cell structure should be uniform from top to bottom and have a fine grain. The crumb color should have good eye appeal and must be characteristic for the cake variety.

The aroma and taste of the cakes should not impart any off-notes when eaten and the mouthfeel should be pleasant, neither dry and crumbly, nor wet and gummy. There should be no lingering aftertaste or unexpected flavor notes or mouthfeel.

Correction of Major Cake Faults

The *peaking* of cakes is caused by pasting of the batter at the sidewall of the pan before all of the chemical leavening has reacted. This is caused by a baking temperature that is too high and is aggravated by a very fluid batter. Lowering the baking temperature by 10-20°F (5.5-11°C) and adding pregelatinized starch (3-5% f.b.) will usually take care of this problem. A more viscous batter will also show less of a "grease ring" on the crust of the cakes. This ring is caused by batter convection from the edge of the pan towards the center.

Cakes with a soft crumb structure and lacking *resilience* need more egg protein. Nonfat dry milk, too, will at least partially help to overcome this problem. Whey solids, however, weaken the crumb structure and will cause it to be more fragile.

An *open grain* structure can have several causes. In most cases, however, it is caused either by too much leavening or too little water. Batters which are under-emulsified or not properly "nucleated" during mixing (insufficient mixing at low speed after creaming) will tend to have an open grain, too. Cakes with a depression at the center and a very open cell structure in that same area, but a denser grain surrounding this open area, require more water. There is not enough water available for the batter to paste properly.

Cakes with a very dense area at the bottom and with a thin firm layer above it (approximately 0.5 inch or 12 millimeters from the bottom) frequently are *over-emulsified*. Here, the emulsifier weakened the crumb structure sufficiently for it to collapse during baking. In white layer cakes this can also be caused by an imbalance in the emulsifier system due to the absence of lecithin normally added with the yolk in whole eggs. The addition of a small amount of lecithin (0.1% f.b.) or of 1% (f.b.) dried whole eggs to the batter may correct this fault in white cakes.

The crumb color of cakes is affected by the pH (acidity) of the system. The presence of reducing sugars, particularly fructose, in combination with a batter pH of 7.8 or higher can cause a *Maillard reaction* (browning reaction) in the crumb. This reaction is most noticeable in the areas pasting first at the bottom and at the periphery of the cake. Conversely, chocolate and devil's food cakes will exhibit a grayish hue in the crumb when the pH of the cake is too low. Significant levels of corn syrup tend to interfere with the development of the reddish pigment in cocoa by buffering the system and keeping the pH of it below 7.8, regardless of how much excess baking soda (sodium bicarbonate) is used in the formula. Chocolate cakes made with high levels of corn syrup will have a brown crumb, but not the desirable reddish brown devil's food cake appearance.

pH Meter

There is no diagnostic instrument that is more useful for establishing the cause of problems in chemically leavened bakery foods than a well maintained and calibrated pH meter. The baker of cakes should always know the pH of the "high-ratio" (chlorinated) cake flour being used. Over-chlorinated and under-chlorinated cake flours are not uncommon and can severely affect the quality of layer cakes. The best pH range for properly chlorinated flours is from 4.7-4.9. However, there have been instances when the flour showed the proper pH, but the cakes had typical symptoms of over- and underchlorination at the same time. This was most likely the result of blending flours with different chlorine treatments.

While under-chlorinated flours produce a weak crumb structure in high-ratio cakes, over-chlorination may cause horizontal cracks in the cake and small radial cracks at the periphery. The problem of over-chlorination can usually be minimized, but not totally eliminated, with increased amounts of cake emulsifier added to the batter.

The pH of a cake batter usually does not predict the crumb pH in the baked cake. Also, the pH of a freshly baked cake may not be the same as the pH of the same cake one day later. Often the pH of prepared food drifts towards neutral (pH = 7). This drift may be quite significant during the first hours after baking, but usually slows to a relatively stable position with time. The farther away the product is from being neutral in acidity, the longer it may take for the pH to stabilize. This holds true not only for cake crumb, but also for soft fillings, such as shelf-stable summer custards (pudding fillings) acidified to a pH of 4.5.

Another factor affecting the pH of cake crumb is the baking temperature. Devil's food cakes baked at a lower temperature (350-360°F or 177-182°C) will tend to be more tender and will have a slightly higher pH than cakes baked from the same batter at 370°F (188°C) or higher. This difference in the pH can also be noticed in the crumb color. The crumb at the bottom of a chocolate cake baked with excessive bottom heat may have a gray cast because of the lower pH in this cake portion. This non-uniformity in crumb pH may lead to inconsistencies in pH determinations.

The crumb pH of typical layer cakes one day after baking should be in the following range:

Yellow Cake: 7.2-7.8 pH
White Cake: 6.8-7.3 pH
Devil's Food Cake: 8-9 pH

The pH of devil's food cakes is usually significantly lower when corn syrup is used in the batter.

Shelf-Life Evaluation

High-ratio layer cakes do not "stale" by the same process as the leaner yeast-leavened products, such as bread and rolls. Cakes stale more rapidly at elevated temperatures than under refrigeration, which is the opposite of what has been observed with bread stored under the same conditions. The mechanism of cake staling is not understood at this time and offers much room for speculation.

Because the staling rate for all baked product is affected by the temperature at which it is stored, it is very important to control the storage temperature for test product. An environmental cabinet is ideal for this purpose, but an air-conditioned room is adequate, provided the product is protected from both cold draft and oven heat alike. It is always recommended to store baked product held for shelf-life evaluation in a closed cabinet to protect it from extreme temperature fluctuations.

Changes in crumb firmness or softness of chemically leavened cakes can be measured with instrumentation much the same as used for bread and rolls. Equipment suitable for measuring crumb deformation by a constant force or the force required to deform crumb in bread by a constant amount will generally also be adequate for cake shelf-life studies. However, the method for measuring the changes may have to be modified slightly. For example, the Method 74-09 of the American Association of Cereal Chemists is modified for cakes by using a slightly smaller (28 millimeter diameter flat bottom) plunger to compress a 1.5 inch (38.1 millimeter) wide strip of cake laid on its side by 4 millimeters (10.5%) at the rate of 50 millimeters per minute. These modified testing parameters were found to yield the desired information about the staling process in chemically leavened layer cakes.

The taste panel procedures for testing cakes is the same as used for bread and rolls. All samples must be coded and presented in a random order.

Conversion to Different Weight Units

In order to convert the following cake formulations from grams to ounces, follow the procedure outlined in Chapter Two, Bread and Roll Baking, (pages 126-129) of this book. By dividing 400 g by 25, the amount of flour used in the cake formulations will be 16 oz. or 1 lb. The 440 g sugar become 17.6 oz. (1 lb., 1 5/8 oz.) etc.

Calculation of Proper Batch Size

In order to obtain reproducible results, it is always best to adjust the batch size to produce sufficient batter to almost or completely cover the mixing agitator after the last addition of liquids (water, eggs, or fruit). The proper batch size can be calculated from the size of the mixing bowl.

The maximum effective capacity of a mixing bowl for mixing cake batters is approximately 80% of its rated volume and a 60% utilization of the bowl volume is still acceptable. To obtain the optimum batch size for a 20 quart (qt.) mixing bowl, do the following calculations for minimum and maximum amounts of batter required:

1. *Effective mixing volume* of 20 qt. bowl: 60-80 %
    0.6 x 20 qt. = 12 qt. minimum
    0.8 x 20 qt. = 16 qt. maximum

2. *Weight of Water* in a volume of 12 (16) qt.:
    1 qt. water weighs approximately 2.09 lbs. or 946 grams (g). Thus:
    12 qt. water weigh 25.0 lbs. or 11356 g
    16 qt. water weigh 33.4 lbs. or 15136 g

3. Want to calculate batch size for **Formula 8** with a specific gravity for the batter of 0.72. Need to know how much *batter weight* is *needed* to fill mixing bowl:

   12 qt. batter: 0.72 x 25.0 lbs. = 18.0 lbs.
   0.72 x 11356 g = 8176 g
   16 qt. batter: 0.72 x 33.4 lbs. = 24.05 lbs.
   0.72 x 15136 g = 10898 g

4. Calculate *amount of flour in batter*. Total ingredient percentage of batter is 393.25% (f.b.). The contribution of flour to the total ingredient percentage is 100% or 1/3.9325 of the batter weight (100% ÷ 393.25%):

12 qt.:	18.0 lbs. ÷ 3.9325 = 4.58 lbs. flour
	8176 g ÷ 3.9325 = 2079 g flour
16 qt.:	24.05 lbs. ÷ 3.9325 = 6.12 lbs. flour
	10898 g ÷ 3.9325 = 2771 g flour

5) *Solution:* Batch size for a 20 quart mixing bowl and a 0.72 specific gravity for **Formula 8** should be based on a weight between 4.5 to 6.125 lbs. (72 to 98 ounces) or 2000 to 2750 g flour.

An experienced baker or baking technologist will need to do only one of the four calculations demonstrated in this example. Whether pounds and ounces or grams are used will depend on the type of scaling device available in the bakery. In most cases it will suffice to calculate only the maximum amount of batter that can be mixed in a particular mixing bowl. The minimum amount can be obtained by multiplying the maximum amount by 0.75 (which is 60% ÷ 80%).

The maximum batch size is especially important for batters that tend to over aerate, while batters that are difficult to aerate should be formulated for batch sizes nearer to the lower limit for the respective mixing bowl. Smaller quantities of batter in a mixing bowl tend to aerate more readily than larger amounts, since more of the agitator is exposed during the creaming stage.

Cake Varieties

There are basically three varieties of high-ratio layer cakes produced in North America:

>Yellow Layer Cake
>White Layer Cake
>Chocolate and Devil's Food Cakes

There are, of course, also other specialty cakes baked as layer cakes, but most are derived from one of the above basic varieties and are rarely produced in baking laboratories as part of a testing program. There is no longer a legal difference between chocolate and devil's food cakes. Chocolate cakes used to be made with melted chocolate liquor and devil's food cakes contained mostly cocoa powder. But because of the difficulty of handling melted chocolate liquor, most bakers discontinued the use of this ingredient in their chocolate cakes.

All three basic cake varieties can be formulated with a wide range of shortening and/or emulsifier levels, which can range from a very small amount of cake emulsifier to more than 50% emulsified shortening based on the flour weight (f.b.). Cakes made with less than 50% (f.b.) emulsified shortening usually require the addition of some cake emulsifier to the batter to enhance their aeration during mixing.

The sugar level in experimental high-ratio layer cake formulations is generally in the range of 110-140% f.b., with 120% being the level most commonly used. The sugar is usually granulated sugar (sucrose). Corn syrups tend to inhibit the aeration of batters and thus cause lower cake volumes. High levels of reducing sugars in corn and invert syrups also result in increased browning of the cake crust and in the crumb via the Maillard reaction. High levels of dextrose may lead to its crystallization (white sugar spots) in the crust and a dry, crumbly texture in the crumb. As mentioned previously, the amount of sugar in the formula also affects the amount of water which must be added to the batter for optimum results.

Since the amount of emulsified shortening in the batter affects the batter's ability to aerate during the mixing process, "leaner" cakes, i.e., cakes made with less shortening, usually require a slightly higher level of chemical leavening than cakes formulated with high shortening levels.

The casein in nonfat dry milk has a beneficial effect on the resilience of the cake crumb which is often not obtained with milk replacers, even though these may contain high levels of whey and protein isolates. Before the 1970s it was common to add 10% (f.b.) nonfat dry milk to cake batters. The present high cost of this ingredient caused many bakers to reduce the level of milk solids in their cake products. This action had little effect on single-layer cakes, but it did create some problems for those bakers who produce multi-layer decorated cakes. The increased tenderness of cakes made with little or no milk causes excessive compression of the bottom layers and undesirable changes in the mouthfeel when they are eaten. Bakers often compensate for this structural weakness by slightly increasing the amount of eggs in the batter.

Yellow Layer Cakes

Yellow layer cakes are made with whole eggs and derive their name from the yellow color imparted by the eggs. However, the diet fed to egg laying chickens today no longer produces the deep yellow color in the egg yolk. Bakers now usually supplement the natural egg color either by adding beta-carotene or "egg shade" food coloring to their batters to create the desired crumb color in yellow layer cakes.

Yellow layer cakes made without shortening are known as *sponge cake*. These cakes are very popular in Western Europe, in the Pacific Rim countries, and in other parts of the world. In these countries, most sponge cakes are still made by the old-fashioned method of whipping the whole eggs with sugar until a stable foam is produced. The flour and other ingredients are then gradually added to the egg/sugar foam and gently incorporated to form a uniform and fluffy batter. The preparation of these batters, however, requires skill and the batter itself tends to lack the stability for mechanical pumping and depositing.

Bakers in North America are using a modified method for making sponge cakes. They simply add 6-6.5% (f.b.) hydrated cake emulsifier (an aqueous dispersion of polysorbate 60, sorbitan monostearate, and monoglycerides) to their sponge cake ingredients and mix the batter with a flat paddle agitator by the regular 4-stage mixing procedure or with a wire whip (whisk) to the desired specific gravity. Significantly less emulsifier is used when the batter is mixed with a continuous batter mixer.

Most yellow layer cakes are, however, made with an emulsified high-ratio cake shortening. The shortening level may range from a low 10% to a high of 60% of the flour weight. As a general rule: the lower the shortening level, the more extra cake emulsifier is added to the batter to facilitate the aeration (nucleation) process during mixing.

The pH range of yellow layer cakes usually lies between the ranges for white and chocolate layer cakes. The relatively dry, resilient crust and crumb of yellow cakes make volume measurements by rapeseed displacement less difficult than for white layer cakes. Thus, yellow layer cakes are usually the first choice of a baking technologist for screening the performance of new ingredients in chemically leavened cakes.

If extended testing becomes necessary, it is advisable to also use other types of cakes with different shortening levels. To evaluate the performance of an ingredient in cakes, the following combination of formulations will, in most cases, provide the desired information about the ingredient's functionality in a broad spectrum of products:

1. Yellow Sponge Cake: 110% (f.b.) sugar, no shortening, but sufficient amount of emulsifier (6-7%). Intermediate pH range (7.2-7.8).
2. White Layer Cake: 140% sugar, 50% emulsified shortening. No cake emulsifier. Lower pH range (7.2 or less).
3. Devil's Food Cake: 120% sugar, 30% emulsified shortening plus cake emulsifier. Higher pH range (8-9.5).

This is, however, an arbitrary selection of formulations and merely a suggestion. A baking technologist in a bakery is advised to use cake formulations actually used by the company. This would definitely be more relevant for future bakery production at the local facility. The same applies to mix manufacturers. But for ingredient development, the formulations suggested above will provide a good starting point.

Cake Formulations

The cake formulations offered in this book have all been test-baked and were found to produce cakes of satisfactory quality with the ingredients used. The baker or baking technologist must, however, be aware of the fact that ingredients may vary slightly from supplier to supplier or change in performance during extended storage. The formulas may, therefore, need slight adjustments for optimum results. Adjustments most often required are in the amount of water added to the batter. Slight increases/decreases in the cake emulsifier and chemical leavening may also be needed.

Formula 8
Yellow Sponge Layer Cake
(110% Sugar)

Baker's Percent	Weight Grams	Ingredients	Mixing Directions
100	400	1) Cake Flour	Mixer: Vertical
110	440	Granulated Sugar	with 5 qt. bowl and
20	80	Dried Whole Eggs	paddle agitator
5	20	Nonfat Dry Milk	
3	12	Pregel. Starch[a]	
2.5	10	Salt	1. Dry-blend ingre-
6	24	Baking Powder[b]	dients. Mix:
6	24	Cake Emulsifier[c]	1 min. = low speed
55	220	2) Water (75°F/24°C)	2. Add liquid. Mix:
0.5	2	Flavoring, BLV[d]	1 min. = low speed
0.25	1	Liquid Egg Color[e]	3 min. = med. speed
40	160	3) Water (75°F/24°C)	3) Add water. Mix:
			1 min. = low speed
			2 min. = med. speed
45	180	4) Water (75°F/24°C)	4) Add water. Mix:
			2 min. = low speed
393.25	**1573**	**Total Amount**	

[a] Pregelatinized waxy maize corn starch.
[b] Double acting baking powder or equivalent amounts of baking soda (30% of weight of baking powder) and sodium acid pyrophosphate (SAPP 28: 41.7% of weight of baking powder).
[c] Dispersion in water of polysorbate 60, sorbitan monostearate, and monoglycerides.
[d] Butter, lemon, and vanilla emulsion.
[e] 3% solution of a blend of Yellow #5 and Yellow #6.

Desired Batter Specific Gravity: 0.67 - 0.72.
Batter Temperature: 72 - 75°F (22 - 24°C).
Scaling Weight: 14 ounces (400 grams) batter per 8 inch (20 centimeter) diameter cake pan.
Bake: At 360°F (182°C) for 25 - 28 minutes (variable) in gas-fired reel oven.
Note: Baking time and temperature may deviate significantly if cakes are baked in convection type ovens.

Formula 9
Yellow Layer Cake
(35% Shortening)

Baker's Percent	Weight Grams	Ingredients	Mixing Directions
100	400	1) Cake Flour	Mixer: Vertical
120	480	Granul. Sugar	with 5 qt. bowl and
20	80	Dried Whole Eggs	paddle agitator
5	20	Nonfat Dry Milk	
2.5	10	Salt	1) Dry-blend ingre-
6	24	Baking Powder[a]	dients. Mix:
3	12	Cake Emulsifier[b]	1 min. = low speed
55	220	2) Water (75°F/24°C)	2) Add liquid. Mix:
0.5	2	Flavoring, Vanilla	1 min. = low speed
0.25	1	Liquid Egg Color[c]	3 min. = med. speed
35	140	Cake Shortening[d]	
40	160	3) Water (75°F/24°C)	3) Add water. Mix:
			1 min. = low speed
			2 min. = med. speed
40	160	4) Water (75°F/24°C)	4) Add water. Mix:
			2 min. = low speed
427.25	**1709**	**Total Amount**	

[a] Double acting baking powder or equivalent amounts of baking soda (30% of weight of baking powder) and sodium acid pyrophosphate (SAPP 28: 41.7% of weight of baking powder).
[b] Dispersion in water of polysorbate 60, sorbitan monostearate, and monoglycerides.
[c] 3% solution of a blend of Yellow #5 and Yellow #6.
[d] Vegetable shortening emulsified with monoglycerides.

Desired Batter Specific Gravity: 0.8-0.84.
Batter Temperature: 72-75°F (22-24°C).
Scaling Weight: 14 ounces (400 grams) batter per 8 inch (20 centimeter) diameter cake pan.
Bake: At 360°F (182°C) for 26-28 minutes (variable) in gas-fired reel oven.
Note: Baking time and temperature may deviate significantly if cakes are baked in convection type ovens.

Formula 10
Yellow Layer Cake
(50% Shortening)

Baker's Percent	Weight Grams	Ingredients	Mixing Directions
100	400	1) Cake Flour	Mixer: Vertical
120	480	Granul. Sugar	with 5 qt. bowl and
20	80	Dried Whole Eggs	paddle agitator
5	20	Nonfat Dry Milk	
2.5	10	Salt	1) Dry-blend ingre-
6	24	Baking Powder[a]	dients. Mix:
3	12	Pregel. Starch[b]	1 min. = low speed
55	220	2) Water (75°F/24°C)	2) Add liquid. Mix:
50	200	Cake Shortening[c]	1 min. = low speed
0.5	2	Flavoring, BLV[d]	3 min. = med. speed
0.25	1	Liquid Egg Color[e]	
40	160	3) Water (75°F/24°C)	3) Add water. Mix:
			1 min. = low speed
			2 min. = med. speed
45	180	4) Water (75°F/24°C)	4) Add water. Mix:
			2 min. = low speed
447.25	1789	Total Amount	

[a] Double acting baking powder or equivalent amounts of baking soda (30% of weight of baking powder) and sodium acid pyrophosphate (SAPP 28·41.7% of weight of baking powder).
[b] Pregelatinized waxy maize corn starch.
[c] Vegetable shortening emulsified with monoglycerides.
[d] Butter, lemon, and vanilla emulsion.
[e] 3% solution of a blend of Yellow #5 and Yellow #6.

Desired Batter Specific Gravity: 0.81 - 0.86
Batter Temperature: 72-75°F (22-24°C)
Scaling Weight: 14 ounces (400 grams) batter per 8 inch (20 centimeter) diameter cake pan.
Bake: At 360°F (182°C) for 26-29 minutes (variable) in gas-fired reel oven.
Note: Baking time and temperature may deviate significantly if cakes are baked in convection oven.

White Layer Cakes

White layer cakes made with 140% (f.b.) sugar have always been considered difficult cakes to make. Method 10-90 of the American Association of Cereal Chemists (AACC) offers a basic cake formulation comprised of 140% (f.b.) sugar and 50% emulsified shortening. This formula is recommended for the evaluation of cake flours. A flour performing well in this test is expected to also perform well in most other cake formulations.

White layer cakes derived their name from their white crumb color. These cakes contain no coloring ingredients and whole eggs are replaced with egg whites (albumen). However, many bakers like to use a small amount of whole eggs in their white layer cakes to gain the benefit of the lecithin in the whole eggs. Even though the amount of lecithin added is minimal, it often causes a significant improvement in the cake quality. Cakes formulated without the benefit of at least 1% (f.b.) whole eggs may have a depression at the center and a collapsed crumb structure near the bottom of the cake. The cakes made without any whole eggs will also be smaller.

The pH of white layer cakes is often reduced to less than 7 by the addition of extra leavening acids (generally known as *cream acid salt*, a mixture of sodium acid pyrophosphate, monocalcium phosphate, and calcium sulfate). This is done to reduce the potential for a browning reaction in the crumb. It is of particular importance for large white cakes which are baked for an extended time, such as wedding cakes.

White cakes are generally bland in flavor and bakers usually add some butter and citrus flavoring to their white batters. Vanilla and almond flavor are also used in white cakes. The baker should, however, avoid the use of a flavor that adds color to the cake crumb, like a very dark vanilla flavor.

Formula 11
White layer Cake
(30% Shortening)

Baker's Percent	Weight Grams	Ingredients	Mixing Directions
100	400	1) Cake Flour	Mixer: Vertical
130	520	Granul. Sugar	with 5 qt. bowl and
1	4	Dried Whole Eggs	paddle agitator
10	40	Egg White Solids	
5	20	Nonfat Dry Milk	
2.5	10	Salt	1) Dry-blend ingre-
7.5	30	Baking Powder[a]	dients. Mix:
5	20	Cake Emulsifier[b]	1 min. = low speed
55	220	2) Water (75°F/24°C)	2) Add liquid. Mix:
30	120	Cake Shortening[c]	
1	4	Flavoring, BLV[d]	1 min. = low speed
0.25	1	Flavoring, Butter	3 min. = med. speed
40	160	3) Water (75°F/24°C)	3) Add water. Mix:
			1 min. = low speed
			2 min. = med. speed
40	160	4) Water (75°F/24°C)	4) Add water. Mix:
			2 min. = low speed
427.25	**1709**	**Total Amount**	

[a] Double acting baking powder or equivalent amounts of baking soda (30% of weight of baking powder) and sodium acid pyrophosphate (SAPP 28: 41.7% of weight of baking powder).
[b] Dispersion in water of polysorbate 60, sorbitan monostearate, and monoglycerides.
[c] Vegetable shortening emulsified with monoglycerides.
[d] Butter, lemon, and vanilla emulsion.

Desired Batter Specific Gravity: 0.72-0.78.
Batter Temperature: 72-75°F (22-24°C).
Scaling Weight: 14 ounces (400 grams) batter per 8 inch (20 centimeter) diameter cake pan.
Bake: At 360°F (182°C) for 25-28 minutes (variable) in gas-fired reel oven.
Note: Baking time and temperature may deviate significantly if cakes are baked in convection oven.

Formula 12
White Layer Cake
(50% Shortening)

Baker's Percent	Weight Grams	Ingredients	Mixing Directions
100	400	1) Cake Flour	Mixer: Vertical
140	560	Granul. Sugar	with 5 qt. bowl and
1	4	Dried Whole Eggs	paddle agitator
10	40	Egg White Solids	
5	20	Nonfat Dry Milk	1) Dry-blend ingre-
2.5	10	Salt	dients. Mix:
7.5	30	Baking Powder[a]	1 min. = low speed
55	220	2) Water (75°F/24°C)	2) Add liquid. Mix:
50	200	Cake Shortening[b]	1 min. = low sped
1	4	Flavoring, BLV[c]	3 min. = med. speed
0.25	1	Flavoring, Butter	
40	160	3) Water (75°F/24°C)	3) Add water. Mix:
			1 min. = low speed
			2 min. = med. speed
45	180	4) Water (75°F/24°C)	4) Add water. Mix:
			2 min. = low speed
457.25	**1829**	**Total Amount**	

[a] Double acting baking powder or equivalent amounts of baking soda (30% of weight of baking powder) and sodium acid pyrophosphate (SAPP 28: 41.7% of weight of baking powder).
[b] Vegetable shortening emulsified with monoglycerides.
[c] Butter, lemon, and vanilla emulsion.

Desired Batter Specific Gravity: 0.85-0.88.
Batter Temperature: 72-75°F (22-24°C).
Scaling Weight: 14 ounces (400 grams) batter per 8 inch (20 centimeter) diameter cake pan.
Bake: At 360°F (182°C) for 24-28 minutes (variable) in gas-fired reel oven.
Note: Baking time and temperature may deviate significantly if cakes are baked in convection oven.

Chocolate and Devil's Food Cakes

Cakes flavored with cocoa can now legally be called *chocolate cake*. For many years, however, cakes made with cocoa were called *devil's food cakes* and only cakes made with chocolate liquor could be labeled "chocolate" cake. Devil's food cakes generally have a reddish-brown crumb in contrast to the dark brown crumb found in chocolate cakes. However, few bakeries are still producing true chocolate cakes and consumers and government agencies have come to accept devil's food cakes as chocolate cakes. Although these two terms are now synonymous and are used interchangeably, very few cakes are labeled as devil's food.

Formula 13
Devil's Food Layer Cake
(30% Shortening)

Baker's Percent	Weight Grams	Ingredients	Mixing Directions
100	400	1) Cake Flour	Mixer: Vertical
120	480	Granul. Sugar	with 5 qt. bowl and
15	60	Dried Whole Eggs	paddle agitator
15	60	Cocoa, Natural	
5	20	Nonfat Dry Milk	
2.5	10	Salt	1) Dry-blend ingre-
3	12	Baking Powder[a]	dients. Mix:
3	12	Baking Soda	1 min. = low speed
4	16	Pregel. Starch[b]	
5	20	Cake Emulsifier[c]	
60	240	2) Water (75°F/24°C)	2) Add liquid. Mix:
30	120	Cake Shortening[d]	1 min. = low speed
0.5	2	Flavoring, Vanilla	3 min. = med. speed
35	140	3) Water (75°F/24°C)	3) Add water. Mix:
			1 min. = low speed
			2 min. = med. speed
40	160	4) Water (75°F/24°C)	4) Add water. Mix:
			2 min. = low speed
438	**1752**	**Total Amount**	

[a] Double acting baking powder or equivalent amounts of baking soda (30% of weight of baking powder) and sodium acid pyrophosphate (SAPP 28: 41.7% of weight of baking powder).
[b] Pregelatinized waxy maize corn starch.
[c] Dispersion in water of polysorbate 60, sorbitan monostearate, and monoglycerides.
[d] Vegetable shortening emulsified with monoglycerides.

Desired Batter Specific Gravity: 0.92-0.98.
Batter Temperature: 72-75°F (22-24°C).
Scaling Weight: 14 ounces (400 grams) batter per 8 inch (20 centimeter) diameter cake pan.
Bake: At 360°F (182°C) for 25-28 minutes (variable) in gas-fired reel oven.
Note: Baking time and temperature may deviate significantly if cakes are baked in convection oven.

Formula 14
Devil's Food Layer Cake
(50% Shortening)

Baker's Percent	Weight Grams	Ingredients	Mixing Directions
100	400	1) Cake Flour	Mixer: Vertical
140	560	Granul. Sugar	with 5 qt bowl and
20	80	Dried Whole Eggs	paddle agitator
20	80	Cocoa, Natural	
10	40	Nonfat Dry Milk	
2.5	10	Salt	1) Dry-blend ingre-
2.5	10	Baking Powder[a]	dients. Mix:
3	12	Baking Soda	1 min. = low speed
3	12	Pregel. Starch[b]	
75	300	2) Water (75°F/24°C)	2) Add liquid. Mix:
50	200	Cake Shortening[c]	1 min. = low speed
0.5	2	Flavoring, Vanilla	3 min. = med. speed
40	160	3) Water (75°F/24°C)	3) Add water. Mix:
			1 min. = low speed
			2 min. = med. speed
50	200	4) Water (75°F/24°C)	4) Add water. Mix:
			2 min. = low speed
516.5	**2066**	**Total Amount**	

[a] Double acting baking powder or equivalent amounts of baking soda (30% of weight of baking powder) and sodium acid pyrophosphate (SAPP 28: 41.7% of weight of baking powder).
[b] Pregelatinized waxy maize corn starch.
[c] Vegetable shortening emulsified with monoglycerides.

Desired Batter Specific Gravity: 0.84-0.88.
Batter Temperature: 72-75°F (22-24°C).
Scaling Weight: 14 ounces (400 grams) batter per 8 inch (20 centimeter) diameter cake pan.
Bake: At 360°F (182°C) for 26-29 minutes (variable) in gas-fired reel oven.
Note: Baking time and temperature may deviate significantly if cakes are baked in convection oven.

CHAPTER

FOUR

Creme Icings and Fillings

The word *creme* implies that the fat phase of the product is aerated during mixing to form a stable foam structure. The term *cream* is reserved for dairy cream only, or for products made from dairy cream, such as whipped cream. Buttercreams are made from butter and this term should never be used for creme icings formulated with regular shortening or margarine.

Although similar in composition, there is a distinct difference between creme icings and creme fillings. Creme fillings are aerated to lower specific gravities than icings and usually have a higher moisture content. There also exists a relationship between the amounts of air and water that can be incorporated into a creme. As a general rule, the more air incorporated into a shortening/sugar mixture, the more water can be incorporated. Fillings and icings can be prepared with either a regular *cake (and icing) shortening* or with a special *icing shortening*. Since these shortenings perform best in the temperature range of 72-77°F (22-25°C), these temperatures also produce the best icings and creme fillings.

Most cake and icing shortenings are actually "high-ratio" shortenings. This type of shortening is emulsified with mono- and diglycerides which form "water in oil" emulsions, i.e., the fat is in the continuous phase (*lipophilic*).

This limits the amount of water that can be added with such fat to less than 75% of the shortening weight (shortening basis, or sh.b.). Consequently, the total amount of moisture that can be added to creme icings and fillings depends on the total amount of shortening in the formula.

Icing shortenings are usually emulsified with more hydrophilic emulsifiers which retain some of the icing or filling in a "fat in water" (*hydrophilic*) emulsion. This not only improves the eating quality of the product, it also tends to have a beneficial effect on the aerating properties of the shortening. This type of emulsification can be achieved either with the addition of 0.1-0.2% (sh.b.) of polysorbate 60 to regular cake shortening emulsified with mono- and diglycerides or by polyglycerol esters of fatty acids used by themselves. Icing shortenings tend to give lower specific gravities in creme icings and fillings and are able to carry up to 90% of their own weight in water.

Creme Icings

Creme icings are used to cover layer cakes and to provide them with a sweet taste and frequently also with a flavor. Icings may be flavored with fruit, vanilla, dairy flavors, and cocoa or chocolate. By incorporating (creaming) air into icings, the baker not only increases the volume of icing, but also improves its eating quality. Because of the increased volume, aerated icings provide more coverage per given weight, but may also be less stable. The most important properties of a "good" cake icing are, however, how easily it can be applied to cakes in a smooth coating and how it retains the appearance of freshness. There are basically two types of creme icings:

1. Decorating Icing
2. Cake Icing

Decorating Icing

The ideal decorating icing is free of air pockets and relatively dry. It must spread easily and form a dry skin at the surface, so that the cake decorator can without difficulty add decorations to the iced cake or food coloring to the icing itself. Decorating icings are usually only lightly aerated to a specific gravity in the range of 0.9-1.1. Their shortening content is about 30% of the sugar weight (s.b.) with a minimum amount of water (about 67% of the shortening weight) and some flavoring and/or food coloring added. Icing shortenings will, in this application, slightly improve the appearance and the eating quality of the icing. Icings made with special icing shortenings usually look smoother, or less "grainy," than similar icings prepared with regular cake and icing shortening.

Many experienced cake decorators smooth the surface of the icing with an icing knife dipped in warm water. This works very well with icings made with regular high-ratio cake shortening. When this is done to icings made with an icing shortening, the very smooth surface created by excessive water added to the continuous water phase will tend to wrinkle as the icing surface dries. It is, therefore, best not to apply this treatment to icings prepared with an icing shortening.

Cake Icing

Aerated (creamed) cake icings are generally applied to cakes without additional decorations. Skilled cake icers usually apply these icings in a pattern. In these applications, total smoothness of the icing surface is generally not desired. In fact, a "textured" icing surface is often preferred. Many iced cakes are garnished, particularly on the sides, with one of a variety of dry toppings, such as minced nut meats, crunches, colored "sprinkles" or flaked coconut.

These creme icings are usually aerated to a specific gravity range of 0.75-0.9. Lower specific gravities often produce large air cells or require special mixing techniques, such as extended mixing at low speed with the mixing bowl filled with the icing above the mixing attachment when the icing reaches the desired specific gravity. Icing shortening is preferred by most bakers for this type of icing. The icing shortening will carry more water (about 75% of its weight) and the icing will remain soft for a longer period of time, even though it forms a thin skin on the surface relatively quickly.

The shortening level for creme icings is significantly higher than for decorating icings. It usually is in the range of 40-70% of the sugar weight, versus 25-35% shortening in decorating icings. As the fat level is increased, it becomes easier to apply this icing in a smooth coat and the icing will remain softer longer. At the higher levels of icing shortening, some butter or margarine may be blended with the shortening for improved flavor. High fat levels also reduce the sweetness of the icing, which may be desirable.

To produce a fruit flavored icing, some of the water may be replaced with pureed fruit or with various specially formulated commercial icing fruits. Citrus fruits (lemon and orange), banana puree, and fruits in season are very popular in cake icings. But fresh fruits often cause a curdled appearance in icings prepared with regular cake and icing shortenings. Icing shortenings are generally more suited for this type of icing.

Because melted chocolate is difficult to add directly to icings, most bakers prefer to use cocoa. But cocoa should always be added either as a paste or in a syrup. Cocoa added to icings as a powder will neither dissolve completely in the fat phase, nor in the water portion of the icing. Commercial cocoa fudge bases are ideal for this application.

But the baker may also prepare his own cocoa fudge base or syrup for icings (See Formula 18).

Creme (plastic) fondant or dry (powdered) fondants can easily be substituted for all or part of the powdered sugar in creme icings. While a direct one-for-one substitution can be made with dry fondant, creme fondant contains only about 88.5% sugar solids and 11.5% moisture, which must be compensated for in the formulation. Therefore, to replace 3000 g powdered sugar, use 3390 g (3000 g divided by 0.885) creme fondant and reduce the amount of water in the formula by 390 g.

Fondant sugar consists of much smaller sugar crystals than powdered sugar (70% of the fondant particles are less than 25 microns in size and 100% are less than 44 microns versus 2% particles in 6X sugar are less than 25 microns in size and only 86.4% are less than 44 microns). While dry fondants contain between 5 and 8% invert sugar, creme fondants usually have some corn syrup added during their manufacture to control the potential growth of sugar crystals. The fructose in the invert sugar holds moisture which gives the icing a sheen. This is not the case with the dextrose portion in the invert sugar or corn syrup. Dextrose is not very soluble at "room temperature" and tends to crystallize as a monohydrate with a dull appearance that does not contribute to the sheen of an icing.

The rich creme icings can also be converted to non-aerated fudge-like icings. Made with about 50-60% (s.b.) icing shortening and some butter or table grade margarine, this type of icing can have an extremely smooth appearance. The high fat content gives excellent spreadability to the icing. However, the lack of air in the product has a softening effect and requires a reduction of water in the formula to about 28-30% of the sugar weight or less than 45% of the total amount of fat (shortening plus fat in margarine or butter). Fudge type icings should be mixed at low speed only. To avoid incorporation of a significant amount of air, their specific gravity is usually between 1.050 and 1.1.

Creme Fillings

Creme fillings are, as their name implies, an aerated filling for layer cakes and particularly for injection into snack cakes. Their shortening level is usually between 45 -60% of the sugar weight and they are aerated to a specific gravity range of 0.45-0.65. Their moisture level ranges from 70-75% of the weight of regular cake shortening, and from 85-95% of the weight of icing shortening. Up to 5% (s.b.) pregelatinized starch is sometimes added to creme fillings to stabilize this component during the shelf-life of the cakes.

Although creme fillings may be flavored like cake icings, most bakers limit themselves to the addition of vanilla and butter flavor. Citrus and chocolate flavored creme fillings, too, enjoy some popularity.

Formula 15
Decorating Icing

Baker's Percent	Weight Grams	Ingredients	Mixing Directions
100	4000	1) Powdered Sugar	1) Combine ingredi-
30	1200	Cake Shortening	ents. Mix:
0.5	20	Salt	1 min. = low speed
5	200	Nonfat Dry Milk	Scrape bowl and mix:
15	600	Water, 86°F (30°C)	3 min. = med.speed
5	200	2) Water (Variable)	2) Add and mix
			smooth:
			15 min. = low speed
155.5	**6220**	**Total Amount**	

Mixer: Vertical mixer with 12 qt. bowl and paddle agitator.
Desired Specific Gravity: 0.90-0.95.
Note: Keep this icing covered to prevent it from forming a dry crust.
Flavors and food coloring may be added to this icing as desired and needed.

Formula 16
Basic Creme Icing

Baker's Percent	Weight Grams	Ingredients	Mixing Directions
100	3000	1) Powdered Sugar	1) Combine ingredi-
30	900	Cake Shortening	ients and mix:
10	300	Table Margarine	1 min. = low speed
0.3	9	Salt	2 min. = med. speed
5	150	Nonfat Dry Milk	
0.7	21	Flavoring, Vanilla	
15	450	Water	
7	210	2) Water	2) Add and mix:
			1 min. = low speed
			5 min. = med. speed
			5 min. = low speed
168	**5040**	**Total Amount**	

Mixer: Vertical mixer with 12 qt. bowl and paddle agitator.
Desired Specific Gravity: 0.75-0.9.

Formula 17
Rich Creme Icing

Baker's Percent	Weight Grams	Ingredients	Mixing Directions
100	3000	1) Powdered Sugar	1) Combine ingred-
50	1500	Icing Shortening	ients and mix:
10	300	Table Margarine	1 min. = low speed
0.3	9	Salt	2 min. = med. speed
20	600	Evaporated Milk	
0.7	21	Flavoring, Vanilla	
5	150	Water (86°F/30°C)	
10	300	2) Water	2) Add and mix:
			1 min. = low speed
			1 min. = med. speed
			5 min. = low speed
196	**5880**	**Total Weight**	

Mixer: Vertical mixer with 12 qt. bowl and paddle agitator.
Desired Specific Gravity: 0.75-0.9.

Formula 18
Cocoa Creme Icing
(Rich)

Baker's Percent	Weight Grams	Ingredients	Mixing Directions
		Basic Creme Icing	
100	3000	1) Powdered Sugar	1) Combine ingredi-
50	1500	Icing Shortening	and mix:
10	300	Table Margarine	1 min. = low speed
0.2	6	Salt	2 min. = med. speed
6	180	Nonfat Dry Milk	
18	540	Water (86°F/30°C)	
		Cocoa Fudge Base	
20	600	2) Water (hot)	2) Combine to form a
12	360	Granulated Sugar	smooth paste and
12	360	Dutched Cocoa	add to Creme Icing. Mix:
			3 min. = low speed
228.2	**6846**	**Total Amout**	

Mixer: Vertical mixer with 12 qt bowl and paddle agitator
Desired Specific Gravity: 0.85-0.95

Formula 19
Rich Creme Filling

Baker's Percent	Weight Grams	Ingredients	Mixing Directions
100	2000	1) Powdered Sugar	1) Combine ingred-
60	1200	Icing Shortening	ients and mix:
0.5	10	Salt	1 min. = low speed
10	200	Nonfat Dry Milk	5 min. = med. speed
1	20	Flavoring, Vanilla	
20	400	Water (77°F/25°C)	
20	400	2) Water	2) Add water and mix:
			1 min. = low speed
			5 min. = med. speed
15	300	3) Water	3) Add water and mix:
			1 min. = low speed
			5 min. = med. speed
			10 min. = low speed
226.5	**4530**	**Total Amount**	

Mixer: Vertical mixer with 12 qt. bowl and paddle agitator.
Desired Specific Gravity: 0.46-0.55.
Note: This creme filling may be injected into snack cakes.

CHAPTER

FIVE

Pound Cakes

Introduction

Pound cakes were probably the original cakes leavened solely with air incorporated during mixing. The pound cake predates all chemically leavened cakes. It is still very popular as a dessert item or as a snack eaten by itself or with ice cream or fruit. The name of this cake is derived from its basic formula:

> 1 lb. Flour
> 1 lb. Sugar
> 1 lb. Salted Butter
> 1 lb. Liquid Whole Eggs

However, few bakers, commercial or home, still use this basic formula. Most pound cakes are made today from "leaner" formulas with less fat and eggs. Today's pound cakes also tend to contain slightly more sugar, chlorinated cake flour, and some optional ingredients, such as water, nonfat dry milk, baking powder, flavoring, and food coloring. In general, ingredients suitable for layer cakes also produce good results in pound and loaf cakes. Loaf cakes are large pound cakes made from a leaner formula with 110% (f.b.) or more sugar and containing a chemical leavener.

Since the basic formula uses neither emulsifiers, nor baking powder, a baker has to resort to special mixing procedures for maximum incorporation of air into the batter. These procedures usually involve creaming (aerating) the butter with some or all of the sugar. Some bakers even whip the eggs with sugar before gently combining all the aerated components with the flour. Most commercial pound cakes are, however, produced by more conventional methods which include the addition of baking powder and emulsifiers.

Mixing of Batter and Formation of Cracks in Crust

There are several methods to produce the desired cracks in the crust of pound cakes, e.g. pulling a spatula (bowl knife) dipped in oil or melted butter through the top of the deposited batter. Whether or not a pound cake "cracks" naturally is often influenced by the mixing method. Pound cake batters well mixed at medium speed (5 minutes) with 40% or less of total water before they are aerated will have less tendency to crack than a batter allowed to cream at the beginning of mixing (with more than 40% of total liquids added). In fact, undermixing of pound cake batters due to excessive creaming in the first mixing stage may cause deep cracks and, in large loaf cakes, also dense collapsed areas in the crumb, particularly near the bottom of the cakes.

The tendency of pound cakes to crack is aggravated by baking conditions. A relatively hot oven (360°F or 182°C) will more likely cause cracking and peaking than a cooler oven set at 325°F (163°C). To obtain a smooth, flat top on the cakes, it is recommended to mix the batter well and with less than 40% of the total liquids (including the liquid in eggs) before creaming and to bake the cakes at the lower end of the temperature range. Conversely, to assure that the crust of the pound cake splits during baking, add more than 50% of the total liquids to the dry ingredients before the first mixing stage. These cakes will tend to split even when baked at 325°F (163°C).

When mixing batters for pound cakes, the baker must keep in mind the size of cake to be produced from this batter. As a general rule, batters for smaller cakes are aerated to lower specific gravities than batters used for larger cakes. While the batter for 14 ounce (400 gram) finished weight pound cakes should be aerated to a specific gravity in the range of 0.78-0.81, the batter for loaf cakes with scaling weights of 55-60 ounces should only be creamed to a specific gravity in the range of 0.85-0.87.

Baking of Cakes

After depositing the batter into greased or paper-lined pans, the cakes should be baked as quickly as possible. The surface of deposited pound cake batter must be protected from drying. Crusting may lead to the formation of sugar crystals, which later become visible as unsightly white spots in the cake crust.

The baking temperature and time for pound and loaf cakes depend not only on the size of the cakes, but also on whether the baker favors a smooth and flat top for cakes, or a peaked and split top. The smaller cakes may be baked for 50 to 60 minutes at 360°F (182°C) when a peaked cake with a split at the center is desired, but the baking time may be extended to 75 or 80 minutes at 325°F (163°C) for cakes with a smooth and flat top. The large loaf cakes are usually baked in special pans insulated with wooden boards on all four sides. Additional insulation is obtained from the corrugated paper pan liners. These cakes may bake as long as two hours at a temperature ranging from 300 to 320°F (150 to 160°C). The actual baking time and temperature for all types of pound cakes may, however, vary significantly for different ovens and pans. When the pound cakes shrink excessively during early stages of cooling, they may benefit from a slight physical shock, such as a slight drop or severe jarring, just as recommended for layer cakes.

Formula 20
Old-Fashioned Pound Cake
(All Butter)

Baker's Percent	Weight Grams	Ingredients	Mixing Directions
100	1000	1) Granul. Sugar	1) Cream butter with
100	1000	Butter[a] (70°F)	sugar. Mix:
			8 minutes = med. speed
100	1000	2) Liquid Whole Eggs	2) Gradually add eggs
			and cream:
			4 minutes = med. speed
100	1000	3) Cake Flour	3) Add remaining in-
2.5	25	Dried Egg Yolk	gredients and mix:
3	30	Salt	1 min. = low speed
1	10	Vanilla	2 min. = med. speed
0.25	2.5	Lemon Emulsion	4 min. = low speed
10	100	Water	
416.75	**4167.5**	**Total Amount**	

[a] Unsalted butter tempered to 70°F (21°C).

Mixer Vertical mixer with 12 qt. bowl and paddle agitator.
Desired Batter Specific Gravity: 0.75-0.78.
Batter Temperature: 68-70°F (20-21°C).
Scaling Weight: 16 ounces (454 grams) batter per PCA #608-35 or PCA #708-45 aluminum foil loaf pan (35 fluid ounces capacity = 1035 cubic centimeters).
Bake: About 55 to 60 minutes at 360°F (182°C) in gas-fired reel oven.
Note: Baking time and temperature may deviate significantly if cakes are baked in convection oven.

Formula 21
Yellow Pound Cake (50% Shortening)

Baker's Percent	Weight Grams	Ingredients	Mixing Directions
100	1000	1) Cake Flour	1) Dry-blend ingred-
120	1200	Granul. Sugar	ients. Mix:
10	100	Nonfat Dry Milk	1 min. = low speed
3	30	Salt	
2	20	Baking Powder[a]	
45	450	2) Liquid Whole Eggs	2) Add eggs, water,
10	100	Water	and shortening. Mix:
1	10	Vanilla	1 min. = low speed
50	500	Cake Shortening	3 min. = med. speed
30	300	3) Water	3) Add liquids. Mix:
0.25	2.5	Lemon Emulsion	1 min. = low speed
0.25	2.5	Liquid Egg Color[b]	2 min. = med. speed
35	350	4) Water	4) Add water and mix:
			3 min. = low speed
406.5	**4065**	**Total Amount**	

[a] Double acting baking powder or equivalent amounts of baking soda (30% of weight of baking powder) and sodium acid pyrophosphate (SAPP 28: 41.7% of weight of baking powder).
[b] 3% solution of a blend of Yellow #5 and Yellow #6.

Mixer: Vertical Mixer with 12 qt. mixing bowl and paddle agitator.
Desired Batter Specific Gravity: 0.78-0.81.
Batter Temperature: 68-70°F (20-21°C).
Scaling Weight: 16 ounces (454 grams) batter per PCA #608-35 or PCA #708-45 aluminum foil loaf pan (35 fluid ounces capacity = 1035 cubic centimeters).
Bake: *Cakes with Natural Split Top:* About 55-60 minutes at 360°F (182°C) in gas-fired reel oven.
  Cakes with Smooth Top: About 75-80 minutes at 325°F (163°C) in gas-fired reel oven.

Note: Baking time and temperature may deviate significantly if cakes are baked in convection oven.
Note: This mixing and baking procedure will produce a pound cake with a good volume and a nice crack.

Formula 22
Devil's Food Pound Cake
(60% Shortening, 10% Butter)

Baker's Percent	Weight Grams	Ingredients	Mixing Directions
100	1000	1) Cake Flour	1) Dry-blend ingre-
125	1250	Granul. Sugar	dients. Mix:
7.5	75	Nonfat Dry Milk	1 min. = low speed
20	200	Cocoa, Dutched	
3	30	Salt	
2.5	25	Baking Powder[a]	
1	10	Baking Soda	
70	700	2) Liquid Whole Eggs	2) Add eggs, water,
30	300	Water	and shortening. Mix:
1	10	Vanilla	1 min. = low speed
60	600	Cake Shortening	5 min. = med. speed
10	100	Butter[b] (70°F)	
25	250	3) Water	3) Add water and mix:
			1 min. = low speed
25	250	4) Water	4) Add water and mix:
			3 min. = low speed
480	**4800**	**Total Amount**	

[a] Double acting baking powder or equivalent amounts of baking soda (30% of weight of baking powder) and sodium acid pyrophosphate (SAPP 28: 41.7% of weight of baking powder).
[b] Unsalted butter tempered to 70°F (21°C)

Mixer: Vertical Mixer with 12 qt. mixing bowl and paddle agitator.
Desired Specific Gravity: 0.78-0.80.
Batter Temperature: 68-70°F (20-21°C).
Scaling Weight: 16 ounces (454 grams) batter per PCA #608-35 or PCA #708 aluminum foil loaf pan (35 fluid ounces capacity = 1035 cubic centimeters).
Bake: About 55 to 60 minutes at 360°F (182°C) in gas-fired reel oven.
Note: Baking time and temperature may deviate significantly if cakes are baked in convection oven.

Cake Muffins

After having almost disappeared from the marketplace during the 1960s, cake muffins made a comeback in the early 1980s with the emergence of special "muffin shops" offering nothing but a wide variety of freshly baked cake muffins. These "gourmet muffins" are much larger than the traditional muffins and their "crowns" spread over the tops of the muffin cups. These crisp muffin tops are now so popular that some muffin shops capitalize on this and offer just *muffin tops* as part of their product mix.

Cake muffins are "low-ratio" chemically leavened sweet goods. They may be topped before baking with a variety of toppings, such as coarse granulated sugar, streusel, crunch, nutmeats, etc.; but muffins are never filled, nor iced with a sweet frosting. Their acceptability by the consumer depends entirely on their image as a wholesome snack and on the flavoring ingredients in the muffin mix. The muffin toppings may enhance the cake's flavor and may also add a "textural sensation" to the mouthfeel.

Cake muffins had their origin in the kitchen and, with the possible exception of chemical leavening, all ingredients used for their production are still readily found in most kitchens. Basic muffin recipes also allow the homebaker to be creative and to use other seasonal ingredients, such as fresh and dried fruits and berries. Muffin batters require minimal mixing and can be quickly prepared. They used to be baked in hot brick ovens immediately following the bread. Cake muffins became special treats for the family on "bread baking days."

When commercial bakeries entered the cake muffin business, butter was replaced with all-purpose shortening or vegetable oil, and nonfat milk solids and water were used in place of liquid whole milk. The sugar level, however, remained generally between 60 and 80% of the flour weight. Pureed and minced fruit, such as bananas and apples, are often added in place of water, while blueberries and cranberries are usually incorporated into the mixed batter as whole berries. When acidic fruits are used, a small amount of baking soda is added to improve the leavening and crust color of the baked product.

Although the fat level in ordinary cake muffins can vary from 10 to 40% of the flour weight, the original cake muffins were often made with very little fat. Commercial bakers gradually increased the fat level to improve the shelf-life of the product. Now, however, bakers are trying to reverse this trend by substituting "fat replacers" for the shortening or vegetable oil in the cake muffin without impairing the shelf-life of the product.

Formula 23
Basic Cake Muffin
(40% Shortening)

Baker's Percent	Weight Grams	Ingredients	Mixing Directions
100	700	1) Bread Flour	1) Dry-blend ingre-
60	420	Granul. Sugar	dients. Mix:
7.5	52.5	Dried Whole Eggs	1 min. = low speed
7.5	52.5	Nonfat Dry Milk	
1.25	8.75	Salt	
5	35	Baking Powder[a]	
55	385	2) Water (75°F/24°C)	2) Add liquid and
40	280	Veget. Shortening[b]	shortening. Mix:
0.5	3.5	Flavoring, Vanilla	1 min. = low speed
27.5	192.5	3) Water (75°F/24°C)	3) Add water. Mix:
			1 min. = low speed
304.25	**2129.75**	**Total Amount**	

[a] Double acting baking powder or equivalent amounts of baking soda (30% of weight of baking powder) and sodium acid pyrophosphate (SAPP 28: 41.7% of weight of baking powder).
[b] All-purpose vegetable shortening.

Mixer: Hobart N-50 with 5 qt. mixing bowl and paddle agitator.
Batter Temperature: 72-75°F (22-24°C).
Scaling Weight: 2.5 ounces (70 grams) batter per 2.75 inch (70 millimeters) top inside diameter muffin pan (Ekco 043) with a capacity of 100 cubic centimeters (cc) per cup.
Bake: At 400°F (205°C) for 19-21 minutes (variable) in gas-fired reel oven.
Note: Baking time and temperature may deviate significantly if muffins are baked in convection oven.

Formula 24
Blueberry Muffin
(40% Vegetable Oil)

Baker's Percent	Weight Grams	Ingredients	Mixing Directions
37.5	225	1) Bread Flour	1) Dry-blend ingre-
60	360	Cake Flour	dients and mix:
85	510	Granul. Sugar	1 min. = low speed
7.5	45	Nonfat Dry Milk	
2.5	15	Salt	
5	30	Baking Powder[a]	
40	240	2) Vegetable Oil	2) Add and incorporate. Mix: 0.5 min. = low speed
55	330	3) Water (cold)	3) Add liquids. Mix
10	60	Liquid Whole Eggs	1 min. = low speed 1 min. = med. speed
Blueberry-Flour Blend			
90	540	4) Wild Blueberries (frozen)	4) Coat berries with flour and incorpo-
2.5	15	Bread Flour	rate into batter[b].
395	**2370**	**Total Amount**	

[a] Double acting baking powder or equivalent amounts of baking soda (30% of weight of baking powder) and sodium acid pyrophosphate (SAPP 28: 41.7% of weight of baking powder).

[b] The frozen flour-coated berries are incorporated into the batter either by mixing at low speed until uniformly dispersed or by folding in with a rubber spatula.

Mixer: Vertical with 5 qt. mixing bowl and paddle agitator.

Scaling Weight: 3 ounces (85 grams) batter per 2.75 inch (70 millimeter) top inside diameter muffin pan (Ekco 043) with a capacity of 100 cubic centimeters (cc) per cup.

Note: Grease top of pan for easy release of baked muffins.

Bake: At 375°F (190°C) for 30-35 minutes (variable) in gas-fired reel oven.

Note: Baking time and temperature may deviate significantly if muffins are baked in convection oven.

Formula 25
Bran Muffin (20% Vegetable Oil)

Baker's Percent	Weight Grams	Ingredients	Mixing Directions
50	500	1) Bread Flour	1) Dry-blend ingre-
30	300	Cake Flour	dients and mix:
20	200	Wheat Bran	1 min. = low speed
60	600	Granul. Sugar	
5	50	Dried Whole Eggs	
2	20	Salt	
1.5	15	Baking Powder[a]	
1.5	15	Baking Soda	
10	100	Dry Honey	
5	50	Dry Molasses	
20	200	Vegetable Oil	
50	500	2) Water	2) Add and mix:
			1 min. = low speed
			1 min. = med. speed
30	300	3) Water	3) Add water and mix
			1 min. = low speed
		Soaked Raisins (30 minutes)	
25	250	4) Seedless Raisins	4) Soak raisins. Add
6	60	Water (80°F/27°C)	to batter and incor-
			porate[b].
316	**3160**	**Total Amount**	

[a] Double acting baking powder or equivalent amounts of baking soda (30% of weight of baking powder) and sodium acid pyrophosphate (SAPP 28: 41.7% of weight of baking powder).

[b] Soaked raisins and all water not absorbed by the fruit are incorporated into the batter by mixing at low speed until all raisins are uniformly dispersed.

Mixer: Vertical with 5 qt. mixing bowl and paddle agitator.

Scaling Weight: 3 ounces (85 grams) batter per 2.75 inch (70 millimeter) top inside diameter muffin pan (Ekco 043) with a capacity of 100 cubic centimeters (cc) per cup.

Note: Grease top of pan for easy release of baked muffins.

Bake: At 380°F (193°C) for 20-25 minutes (variable) in gas-fired reel oven.

Note: Baking time and temperature may deviate significantly if muffins are baked in convection oven.

Formula 26
Corn Muffin
(25% Vegetable Shortening)

Baker's Percent	Weight Grams	Ingredients	Mixing Directions
100	800	1) Bread Flour	1) Dry-blend ingre-
35	280	Corn Meal, Coarse	dients and mix:
70	560	Granul. Sugar	1 min. = low speed
10	80	Nonfat Dry Milk	
10	80	Dried Whole Eggs	
2.5	20	Salt	
7.5	60	Baking Powder[a]	
25	200	2) Veget. Shortening	2) Add and mix:
65	520	Water	1 min. = low speed
			1 min. = med. speed
30	240	3) Water	3) Add water. Mix:
			2 min. = low speed
355	**2840**	**Total Amount**	

[a] Double acting baking powder or equivalent amounts of baking soda (30% of weight of baking powder) and sodium acid pyrophosphate (SAPP 28: 41.7% of weight of baking powder).

Mixer: Vertical with 5 qt. mixing bowl and paddle agitator.
Scaling Weight: 3 ounces (85 grams) batter per 2.75 inch (70 millimeter) top inside diameter muffin pan (Ekco 043) with a capacity of 100 cubic centimeters (cc) per cup.
Note: Grease top of pan for easy release of baked muffins.
Bake: At 380°F (193°C) for 20 to 25 minutes (variable) in gas-fired reel oven.
Note: Baking time and temperature may deviate significantly if muffins are baked in convection oven.

CHAPTER

SEVEN

Cake Doughnuts

Introduction

Cake doughnuts are one of the most difficult bakery items to produce in the laboratory or in a small bake shop. The only suitable small-scale automated cake doughnut depositors and fryers use gravity-fed depositors, while much of the equipment used by large doughnut manufacturers utilizes vacuum or pressure for depositing doughnut batters. The old pressure-fed DCA (Doughnut Corporation of America)

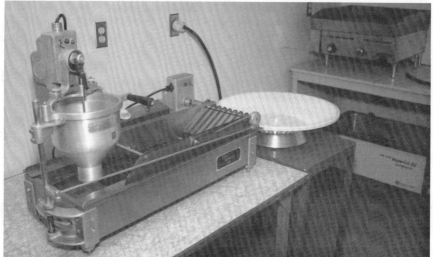

A gravity-fed doughnut depositor.

Belshaw doughnut fryer. (Photo Courtesy of Belshaw Equipment Co.).

Belshaw SpaceSaver™ automatic doughnut product system. (Photo Courtesy of Belshaw Equipment Co.).

Lincoln automatic doughnut machines have been almost entirely phased out and any still in operation are relics of another era.

Because of the complexity of doughnut mixes, very few doughnut manufacturers produce this product from "scratch" by weighing and blending individual ingredients. Most bakers buy doughnut mixes formulated according to their specifications regarding fat absorption, crumb tenderness, and flavor profile. Mixes not only simplify the manufacturing process of doughnuts, but also significantly reduce the number of ingredients the bakery must keep in inventory.

Doughnut Ingredients

Doughnut flour is usually a blend of approximately 70% flour milled from soft red wheat and 30% flour milled from hard red wheat. The formulation contains about 40% (f.b.) or slightly less granulated sugar. The more sugar in the mix, the less water is added and the more fat will be absorbed by the doughnut during frying. Since granulated sugar is not a reducing sugar like dextrose, fructose, and lactose and cannot participate in Maillard reactions (browning taking place in the crust during baking or frying), it is customary to also add 2% (f.b.) dextrose to doughnut batters for an improved crust color. Nonfat milk solids, too, aid in crust color development. Milk protein not only contributes to the Maillard reaction, the casein, which comprises about 80% of the total milk protein, also helps to reduce fat absorption.

Because doughnut production proceeds at a very fast rate, the batter dropped into the hot fat during depositing must rise to the surface very quickly so it can be moved on by the "flights" (moving bars attached to two travelling chains) travelling at the fat's surface, or the next batter deposit will be dropped on top of the previously deposited doughnut. For this reason doughnut formulations specify a fast acting leavening acid, such as sodium acid pyrophosphate #40 or # 43 (doughnut pyrophosphate).

Moisture in Doughnuts

Another ingredient affecting general doughnut quality is the water. Part of the water near the doughnut surface is transformed into steam and this steam prevents frying fat from being absorbed by the doughnut. After the steam has escaped, the doughnut starts absorbing frying fat. There is an inverse relationship between moisture retention by the doughnut during frying and the amount of fat absorbed by the product. The more water in the doughnut batter, the less fat the doughnut tends to absorb during frying. However, too much water in the doughnut batter (i.e., a soft batter) will cause the doughnuts to spread more than desired and be misshaped. To correct this batter viscosity problem, a small amount of a soluble gum (CMC [Carboxymethylcellulose], xanthan gum, etc.) is usually added to restore the optimum batter viscosity for the desired symmetrical doughnut shape. Good results have also been obtained with the addition of 1-3% (f.b.) powdered cellulose (110 micron length) to doughnut batters.

A high residual moisture content in the doughnut can, however, cause problems with doughnut coatings. Coating sugar can draw moisture from the doughnut through their difference in water activity. This can cause the sugar to gradually transform into a wet and slimy paste. Since dextrose monohydrate is less soluble and thus more stable at room temperature than powdered sugar, powdered dextrose is usually used for coating all types of baked and fried sweet goods. A high moisture content in doughnuts is also often responsible for the breakdown of confectioner's chocolate coatings, which contain up to 50% regular sugar (sucrose).

Batter Mixing and Processing

The proper mixing of doughnut batters is very important. During this process, the ingredients are combined, hydrated, and transformed into a viscous mass. Even though gluten development in chemically leavened sweet goods is not a critical factor, undermixed and overmixed cake doughnut batters will not produce quality doughnuts. Doughnut batters usually require a hydration (rest) time of about 10 minutes and, for best results, must be processed within 30 to 35 minutes after mixing. Doughnuts made from improperly hydrated batters have poor symmetry and shape. The batter should not be allowed to hydrate in the warm hopper of a depositor mounted above the hot frying fat. Although some manufacturers of commercial doughnut mixes may recommend warmer batter temperatures, most bakers try to control their doughnut batter temperatures in the range of 76-80°F (24.5-26.5°C).

In contrast to cakes which lose weight during baking (9 to 10% bake-out loss), doughnuts gain weight through fat absorption during frying. Whereas a cake doughnut batter may contain 2.5-3% fat as vegetable oil or shortening, fried doughnuts usually consist of 20-30% fat and 18-25% moisture. As mentioned earlier, these two components generally have an inverse relationship, and doughnuts with a high residual moisture level usually have a low fat absorption and vice versa.

Frying Fat

The fat used for doughnut frying should be of a good quality. Vegetable oils will deteriorate rapidly during frying through hydrolysis and polymerization. These changes are easily recognized as "smoke" and foam formation during frying. Products fried in oil also feel and look "oily." Partially hydrogenated frying fats will resist deterioration during frying and will not leave an oily film on the product. It is for these reasons that nonhydrogenated domestic vegetable oils are not recommended for frying bakery foods.

Frying fats with a relatively low solids content (less than 8%) at 104°F (40°C) may also cause problems when the product is coated with sugar or a confectionery chocolate coating. The powdered coating sugar tends to absorb oil from the product surface and will compact during processing and turn an unsightly grayish yellow. The confectioner's coating, too, will absorb surface oil into its own fat matrix and cause it to break down and soften. For these reasons, a partially hydrogenated vegetable frying fat with 10 to 15% solids at 104°F (40°C) is recommended for doughnut manufacture.

Doughnut Frying

The optimal frying temperature is between 360-370°F (182-188°C). Lower temperatures will increase the fat absorption by the doughnut, and higher temperatures will accelerate the breakdown of the fat. The addition of the antifoaming agent dimethylpolysiloxane (also known as *methyl silicone*) to doughnut frying fats is not recommended. Doughnuts fried in fat containing methyl silicone are of inferior quality and tend to have a poor crust color with blotchy areas.

Fat, as it breaks down, will darken in color and increase in viscosity. This will eventually lead to foaming, off-flavors, and smoking. When the frying fat has deteriorated to this degree, it should be discarded. A broken down frying fat not only has an adverse effect on doughnut quality (e.g. off-flavor and dark crust color), but it also endangers the safety of employees working at or near the frying equipment. They are exposed to the fumes and the foaming fat may cause severe burns. Broken down fat should also never be added to fresh fat. The break-down products of fats and oils catalyze (accelerate) further deterioration of heated fat!

Care of Frying Fat

Although a large doughnut manufacturer frying goods almost continuously and filtering the fat frequently seldom needs to discard broken down frying fat, small bakeries can extend the life of their fat by lowering the temperature of the fryer when it is not used and by periodically passing the fat through a filter woven from cotton or some other heat resistant fabric. There are also filtering devices available which pass the hot fat through a filter compound, usually consisting of diatomaceous earth or a synthetic calcium silicate. These are the same filtering compounds used by the shortening industry for bleaching fats after they have been refined.

It is not only important to remove the charred particles from the hot fat, but also to avoid contamination of the fat with metallic particles and soaps or detergents. Trace amounts of copper, brass, bronze, and iron can significantly shorten the useful life of even the best quality fat. The use of copper or brass fittings (e.g. valves and tubing to convey hot fat) and utensils must be avoided in all frying operations!

Formula 27
Basic Cake Doughnut

Baker's Percent	Weight Grams	Ingredients	Mixing Directions
70	1120	1) Cake Flour	1) Blend dry ingredi-
30	480	Bread Flour	ents:
40	640	Granulated Sugar	1 min. = low speed
2	32	Dextrose	
7.25	116	Nonfat Dry Milk	
9.375	150	Egg Yolk Solids	
2.25	36	Salt	
1.5	24	Baking Soda	
2.063	33	Sodium Acid Pyro-phosphate (SAPP 40)	
0.25	4	Nutmeg	
0.156	2.5	Mace	
6.25	100	2) All-Purp. Shortening	2) Add liquids and shortening. Incor-
0.5	8	Vanilla	porate and mix:
64.25	1028	Water	1 min. = low speed
			2 min. = med. speed
235.844	3773.5	Total Amount	

Mixer: Vertical mixer with 12 qt. mixing bowl and paddle agitator.
Batter Temperature: 76-78°F (24.5-25°C).
Rest Time: 10 minutes under ambient conditions.
Depositor: Automated doughnut depositor and fryer.
Doughnut Cutter Size: 1.5 inch (38 millimeter) diameter.
Weight of Fried Doughnut: 1.3 to 1.5 ounces (37-42 grams).
Frying Temperature: 365-370°F (185-188°C).
Frying Time: 90 to 94 seconds (45 seconds to turnover).
Note: It is very important that the fryer is level and always filled to the proper level with frying fat. Low fat levels may cause freshly dropped doughnuts to temporarily stick to the drop-plate and to become misshaped.
Note: It is recommended that the frying equipment is operated under a ventilated hood.

CHAPTER EIGHT

Sweet Dough

Introduction

Cakes prepared from yeast-leavened sweet doughs have been favorite treats long before chemical leavening became available. They were often topped with ripe fresh fruit and/or a melt-away streusel topping. Although honey was most likely the original sweetener used in sweet doughs and toppings, this ingredient was gradually replaced with granulated sugar when it became available and affordable during the 19th century.

Sweet dough is essentially a bread dough with extra sugar (originally honey) and fat added to it. Since the extra sugar tends to slow down yeast activity, the amount of yeast added to sweet doughs is usually increased proportionately to control the fermentation time. Because higher sugar levels and the extra fat tend to soften doughs, a reduction in the amount of water added to the dough is usually necessary.

Formulation

A bread flour with about 11-12% protein is generally preferred for sweet doughs. A dough prepared with this flour will support a fair amount of topping and will produce a baked product with a good eating quality. Doughs prepared from preferments (sponge) or fermented straight doughs sometimes lack extensibility during make-up. In such doughs bakers often replace 10-20% of the bread flour with pastry flour to produce a slightly more extensible gluten matrix and a more tender crumb structure.

Sweet doughs may contain as little as 8% sugar, or as much as 22% or more based on the total flour weight. The sugar may be in the form of granulated sugar (sucrose) or as solids in 42% high fructose corn syrup (71% solids). The amount of fat varies in a similar range. Nonfat milk has generally been replaced with either whey solids or with a milk replacer at the 2.5-5% (f.b.) level. Many bakers add some whole eggs to their sweet doughs. The amount ranges from 10% (f.b.) for cinnamon rolls to a liberal amount of 20% liquid whole eggs (75% moisture content) in rich sweet doughs. Dried whole eggs may be used in place of liquid or frozen eggs without affecting the flavor of the finished product.

Monoglycerides are not only added as crumb softeners, but they may also help to control the "popping" of cinnamon rolls baked in a cluster. This phenomenon is caused by excessive expansion of the dough during the early stages of baking, which forces the inside of a coiled dough piece upwards. Popping can be reduced by using twice the normal amount or more of a monoglyceride crumb softener in the sweet dough.

Most bakers add liquid egg color to their doughs to improve the eye appeal of the baked product. Mineral yeast food, however, is added only to preferments and rarely to straight doughs. Dough strengtheners and oxidation are usually reserved for doughs subjected to physical stress, such as extruded doughs, and are rarely used in doughs subjected to manual make-up.

Mixing

Sweet doughs in baking laboratories and small bakeries are usually mixed with a dough hook in the bowl of a vertical mixer. A full gluten development in the dough will result in a well-expanded product, but it will also reduce the extensibility of the dough during make-up and may cause *popping* of cinnamon rolls baked in a cluster. Most bakers mix their doughs only to the "clean-up" stage where the dough has formed one cohesive mass.

A dough temperature of 80-82°F (27-28°C) is recommended. Sweet doughs may be processed with only 10 minutes fermentation time under ambient conditions (floor time), or they may be divided into 8-15 lb. pieces and retarded (kept under refrigeration at 41-45°F or 5-7°C) for processing at a later time. While retarding, the dough pieces must be protected from drying out.

Fermentation

Fermentation of sweet doughs will improve the flavor and shelf-life of the finished product. It may also significantly reduce the dough's extensibility which may cause difficulties during make-up and "popping" in rolls during baking. Replacing 10-20% of the bread flour with pastry flour will significantly reduce or eliminate the adverse effects of fermentation.

Make-Up

Sweet dough may be processed either into individual rolls or into larger units, such as coffee cakes. The quality of the baked product is generally dependent on the amount and type of filling and/or topping used with the dough. While smears and fruit fillings are most popular, dry and granular fillings are difficult to keep in place during the continuous make-up of dough pieces.

Sweet Rolls

The most common continuous make-up procedure for sweet rolls consists of sheeting the dough into a long strip 9-11 inches (23-28 centimeters) wide and about 3/16 inch (5 millimeters) thick. The filling is then uniformly spread over the entire dough strip, leaving only the bottom 1/2 inch (12 millimeters) free of filling. The filled dough strip is then rolled into a long cylinder, also known in the industry as *snake*, starting from one corner at the top. The filled dough is rolled across the shorter distance (9 inches or 22.5 centimeters) of the dough piece and sealed at the bottom. The 2.25 inch (57 millimeters) diameter dough cylinder is then adjusted to uniform thickness and sliced with a sharp metal blade (bench scraper or knife) into pieces weighing 1.75-2 ounces (49-56 grams) each. The filled pieces are then properly spaced in a greased pan, in an aluminum foil pan, or on a paper-lined aluminum sheet pan with a cut side of the dough piece facing up. Nine dough pieces fill an 8 by 8 inch (20 by 20 centimeters) square aluminum pan (PCA 664-35).

An excellent cinnamon roll can be produced from the following formulation:

Cinnamon Rolls

100% Sweet Dough (Formula: 28, 29, or 30*)
12% Cinnamon Smear (Formula 31)
5% Baking or Conditioned Raisins

* Note: Although Formula 30 (Cinnamon Roll Dough) produces a stronger and very elastic dough with a better taste in the baked product, the rolls tend to "pop" (center curl pushes up) during baking. Unfermented straight doughs

Dough strip sheeted and filled.

Dough snake divided into individual pieces for clustered cinnamon rolls.

Baked clusters of cinnamon rolls.

Iced clusters of cinnamon rolls.

Filled dough strips twisted and coiled into "snails."

mixed only to the "pick-up" stage are more extensible and easier to sheet and make-up into rolls that will not produce "popping."

The average baking time for cinnamon rolls is 16-18 minutes at 400°F (205°C) in a gas-fired reel oven.

A more tedious make-up for sweet rolls is still popular with small retail shops. This make-up requires that the dough be sheeted to a uniform thickness of about 1/2 inch (12 millimeters) and cut into strips weighing approximately 2 ounces (56 grams). The dough may be filled for extra flavor with 10-15% (based on dough weight) filling, such as a melt-away filling (Formula 33), pecan crunch filling (Formula 34), or an almond filling (Formula 36). The filled strips are twisted and coiled into *snails*, double snails, or into an S-shaped configuration.

After proofing, the sweet rolls are egg-washed and

Twisted dough strips shaped into snails, double snails, and "S" configuration.

Sweet rolls proofed and topped with cinnamon crunch or apple topping.

Sweet rolls baked and iced.

topped either with a streusel, crunch, or a fruit topping. The average baking time for these rolls is 15-17 minutes at 400°F (205°C) in a gas-fired reel oven. While rolls topped with streusel or crunch are usually "swirl-iced" (fine strands of icing swirled on product), fruit-topped rolls are often "spot-iced" by applying the icing only to the highest parts of the rolls.

Coffee Cakes

There are three basic make-up methods for coffee cakes. One is similar to that used for sweet rolls. The dough is filled with 12-20% of its weight of a flavored smear and is curled into a cylinder with a diameter of not more than 2 inches (5 centimeters) and cut to the desired length. The filled long dough piece is then cut lengthwise with a scraper and the cut surfaces of the split pieces are turned up and exposed when they are placed in an oblong baking tray

Filled and partially rolled up dough snake for coffee cakes.

A split dough snake piece braided into a coffee cake shape.

A dough piece being split for shaping into a coffee cake.

(PCA 6002-30) or on a paper-lined aluminum sheet pan (*split snake* make-up). The cut pieces may also be twisted or braided together to produce a more unique shape.

The dough piece may also be cut all the way through except for a half inch (12 millimeter) at both ends. The two halves may then be spread and shaped into an oval ring, or into the shape of a heart. An alternate make-up for a ring coffee cake is to make cuts about one inch apart through half of the dough cylinder and to form a ring from it with the serrated edge facing the outside.

Another attractive make-up shape for coffee cakes is the *scissor cut*. After the dough piece is placed in the oblong coffee cake pan, deep cuts are made with a pair of scissors 1-1.25 inches (25-32 millimeters) apart and at a 30° angle. The cut sections are then spread into opposite directions. The appearance of the finished product gives rise to the alternate name for this type of make-up, the

A split dough piece formed in the shape of a heart.

Dough piece being serrated for a ring coffee cake.

A ring coffee cake.

An assortment of proofed coffee cakes ready for topping.

Baked coffee cakes.

Iced coffee cakes.

Coffee cakes ready for "scissor cutting."

Make-up of "scissor-cut" coffee cakes.

Proofed "scissor cut" coffee cakes ready for topping with cinnamon crunch.

Baked and iced "scissor cut" coffee cakes.

alligator cut. The average baking time for these coffee cakes is 18-20 minutes at 400°F (205°C) in a gas-fired reel oven.

Small bakeries often lack the equipment and the facilities to sheet dough pieces into long strips. Under these conditions it is best to divide the sweet dough into individual pieces weighing 12 ounces (340 grams). After rounding, the dough pieces are placed on a flour-dusted sheet pan and covered with a cloth to protect them from drying. The pieces may be allowed to relax for a few minutes or may be refrigerated for make-up at a later time.

During make-up, these dough pieces are flattened and shaped with a wooden pie pin into 7 x 11 inch (18 x 28 centimeter) rectangles. One half of the area of each dough piece is covered with a filling (either a smear or a fruit pie filling with a relatively high solids content). The bare portion of the dough piece is then folded over the filling and sealed at the two ends. After panning, slits are cut into the top dough layer to allow the steam to escape from the filling during baking. These coffee cakes may be baked either on a paper-lined aluminum sheet pan or in an aluminum foil pan (12.375 x 5.375 x 1 inch or 31.43 x 13.65 x 2.42 centimeter PCA 6002-30 Danish coffee cake pan). The baking time ranges from 19-21 minutes at 400°F (205°C) in a gas-fired reel oven.

The following fillings produce excellent coffee cakes with 12 ounces (340 grams) sweet dough:

Cream Cheese Filling .... 5 oz. (142 grams)
Fruit Pie Filling .... 6 oz. (170 grams)
Almond Filling (Formula 36) .... 3 oz. (85 grams)

The combination of 3 oz. (85 g) cream cheese filling and 4 oz. fruit pie filling is very popular. However, other

Shaping of 12 g dough pieces for coffee cakes.

Spreading of filling over half of dough piece.

Filled dough piece placed in coffee cake pan.

Coffee cake with venting cuts ready for proof box.

types of fillings also find very good acceptance with customers.

In order to improve the appearance of the baked coffee cakes, they should be washed after proofing with a mild egg wash (50% liquid whole eggs + 50% cold water with a pinch of salt) at the rate of 1/10 oz. or 2.8 grams per coffee cake. They are then topped with 3/4 oz. (21 grams) streusel (Formula 38,39) or with a crunch (Formula 40) topping. After baking, the cakes should be "iced" with 1.5-2 oz. (42-56 grams) of sweet roll icing (Formula 37).

The third method for making coffee cakes requires sheeting the large dough piece into a long 18-20 inch wide (45 to 50 centimeter) strip about 1/4 inch (6 millimeters) thick. A relatively dry, but spreadable, smear (15-20% filling based on dough weight) is spread over the lower half of the dough strip and covered with the bare top half of the dough sheet to yield a filled dough piece 9-10 inches

Spreading of filling over half of dough sheet.

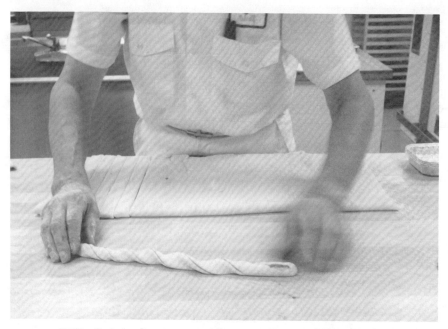

Filled dough piece cut into strips to be twisted.

Twist coffee cakes ready for the proof box.

Twist coffee cakes topped with fruit or cinnamon crunch.

(22-25 centimeters) wide and about 1/2 inch (12.5 centimeters) thick. This filled dough piece is then cut into narrow strips weighing 4-4.5 ounces (110-125 grams). Three of these strips are twisted and placed parallel to each other into an oblong baking tray (PCA 6002-30). Individual smaller filled and twisted strips (2-2.5 ounces or 55-70 grams) can be coiled into *snails* and baked as sweet rolls.

After proofing, the coffee cakes are egg-washed and topped with 3/4 oz. (21 grams) streusel or a crunch. Cakes filled with a cinnamon flavored filling may also be topped with about 4 oz. (113 grams) apple topping extruded in two strands between the twisted dough strips.

Fillings

Although moist (viscous) fillings generally have a better eating quality, wet (fluid with or without chunky components) fillings do not produce desirable sweet goods. Some of the water becomes steam during baking and if the steam is not properly vented, it will cause a large cavity inside the pastry. The steam will also saturate the dough next to the filling and cause it to cook rather than bake. This produces an undesirable mouthfeel and should be avoided. For this reason, the moisture content in pastry fillings must be controlled.

To improve the spreadability of fillings, a small amount of vegetable oil may be added to them in place of water. Liquid egg whites will accomplish the same, since the egg albumen (protein in egg whites) binds the moisture of the egg white when the egg white coagulates during baking. The moisture in egg whites does not form a significant amount of steam. It is, however, recommended that all moist fillings be vented during baking by exposing part of the filling to the environment by the type of make-up used or through cuts in the top crust of the dough piece. As a general rule: the more moisture in the filling, the more exposed it must be! Unvented steam causes cavities in bakery foods during baking.

Although most large bakeries formulate and produce their own coffee cake and sweet roll fillings and toppings, small shops have available to them a vast variety of these products from commercial sources. Their quality ranges from fair to excellent and their large selection and shelf-stability makes it easier for retail bakeries to offer their customers a wide variety of bakery foods.

Toppings

There are two basic types of toppings used for sweet rolls and coffee cakes:

1. Streusels and crunches
2. Fruit, jellies, and jams.

Streusels and Crunches

The streusels and crunches consist of three basic ingredients: sugar, fat, and flour. The sugar not only gives the desirable sweet taste to the topping, but it also contributes to the topping's "crunchy" mouthfeel and helps to make the topping more crumbly to facilitate its application. While granulated sugar is usually used for crunches, powdered sugar performs better as a drying agent in streusels made with a relatively high fat content.

The fat "binds" the basic ingredients together into small lumps which can be easily spread over the surface of sweet rolls and coffee cakes. The more fat in the mix, the better the eating quality of the topping. "Melt-away" streusels contain a relatively large amount of fat. Baking margarines are usually preferred as fat for these toppings, as they contribute extra flavor to the product. Butter, too, is an ideal fat for streusels, but its cost precludes its use by many bakers. Also, butter streusels must be processed and stored at lower temperatures (59-68°F or 15-20°C) than similar products made with a baking margarine. Because of their softness, table-grade margarines usually require larger amounts of flour in the formula to preserve the "crumbliness" of the topping than when the firmer baking margarines are used. Crunches are formulated with less fat and with more sugar relative to the amount of flour used in streusels.

The flour's main function in a streusel or crunch is to act as a drying ingredient to prevent excessive clumping during storage or application of the topping. Excessive use of flour, however, must be avoided, since the flour has an adverse effect on the eating quality of the topping and some clumping of the ingredients is desirable.

Vanilla and citrus flavors are frequently added to streusels to enhance the taste of the pastry. Crunches are often formulated with brown sugar in place of regular granulated sugar and are flavored with spices. This category of toppings may also contain nutmeats and other components to add taste and textural qualities to the finished product.

Fruit Toppings

Fresh fruit finds only limited use for topping coffee cakes and pastries. Their high water activity can cause microbial spoilage within a few days. Fruits should, therefore, be processed into toppings with a high sugar content to prevent them from boiling during baking and also from microbial spoilage before consumption. Although small chunks of fruit are desirable in toppings, the pieces should not be so large that they interfere with depositing or cause an irregular distribution on the product. Fruit toppings that boil during baking have been formulated with too little sugar. Sugar raises the boiling point of the liquid in the topping and it also lowers its water activity, thus reducing moisture loss during baking and storage.

Proofing and Baking

Regular sweet dough pastries and coffee cakes are fully proofed before baking, i.e., they leave a very slight indentation where touched. Sweet dough items are also baked "hot and fast" in a temperature range of 385-420°F (195-215°C). The smaller individual pastries are baked at the higher temperature, while the coffee cakes with heavy fillings are baked longer at the lower temperature. Cluster rolls are baked at an intermediate temperature.

Formula 28
Basic Sweet Dough

Baker's Percent	Weight Grams	Ingredients
100	4000	Bread Flour (11.5% Protein)
16	640	Granulated Sugar
2.5	100	Nonfat Dry Milk or Milk Replacer
2	80	Salt
8	320	Soybean Oil
1	40	Crumb Softener (Monoglycerides)
6	240	Compressed Yeast
0.1	4	Liquid Egg Color (3% Solution)
52	2080	Water and Ice (Variable)
187.6	**7504**	**Total Amount**

Mixer: Vertical mixer with 20 quart bowl and dough hook.
Mixing: Mix at medium speed until dough has "cleaned" the mixing bowl and formed a cohesive mass.
Dough Temperature: 80-82°F (27-28°C).
Fermentation (Rest) Time: 10 minutes under ambient conditions.
Note: Dough may also be divided without delay and retarded for make-up at a later time.
Note: If sweet rolls or coffee cakes prepared from this dough show signs of a collapsed dough structure below a heavy filling or topping, add 5% (f.b.) dried whole eggs to the dough or reduce the amount of filling.

Formula 29
Rich Sweet Dough

Baker's Percent	Weight Grams	Ingredients
100	4000	Bread Flour (11.5% Protein)
22	880	Granulated Sugar
2.5	100	Nonfat Dry Milk or Milk Replacer
1.5	60	Salt
22	880	All-Purpose Shortening
2	80	Crumb Softener (Monoglycerides)
9	360	Compressed Yeast
0.1	4	Liquid Egg Color (3% Solution)
16	640	Liquid Whole Eggs
36	1440	Water and Ice (Variable)
211.1	**8444**	**Total Amount**

Mixer: Vertical mixer with 20 quart bowl and dough hook.

Mixing: Mix at medium speed until dough has "cleaned" the mixing bowl and formed a cohesive mass. Gluten development will toughen the dough.

Dough Temperature: 80-82°F (27-28°C).

Fermentation (Rest) Time: 10 minutes under ambient conditions.

Note: Dough may also be divided without delay and retarded for make-up at a later time. Fermentation will improve the flavor and toughen the dough.

Formula 30
Cinnamon Roll Dough
(Sponge and Dough Method)

Baker's Percent	Weight Grams	Ingredients
	Sponge: (Preferment)	
60	2400	Bread Flour (11.5% Protein)
0.5	20	Mineral Yeast Food
3	120	Compressed Yeast
36	1440	Water
	Dough: (Remix)	
40	1600	Bread Flour (11.5% Protein)
20	800	42% High-Fructose Corn Syrup
2.5	100	Nonfat Milk Solids
1.8	72	Salt
2.5	100	Dry Whole Eggs
10	400	Bread Shortening
3.5	140	Compressed Yeast
0.1	4	Lemon Emulsion
0.1	4	Liquid Egg Color (3% Solution)
7	280	Water and Ice (Variable)
187	**7480**	**Total Amount**

Mixer:	Vertical mixer with 20 quart bowl and dough hook.
Sponge:	*Fermentation Time:* 3-4 hours at 84°F (24-25°C). *Temperature:* 74-77°F (24-25°C).
Dough:	*Mix:* At medium speed until dough has "cleaned" the mixing bowl and formed a cohesive mass. If dough is not extensible enough, replace up to 20% of the bread flour with pastry flour. *Temperature:* 78-80°F (25.5-26.5°C).
Floor Time:	10-15 minutes under ambient conditions.
Make-up:	Sheet dough piece to desired size and thickness and cover with 75 grams vegetable oil (1% of dough weight) and 375 grams of a *Cinnamon Sugar* mixture (5% of dough weight) or with 900 grams *Cinnamon Smear* (12% of dough weight). Roll up (curl) filled dough piece into a long cylinder (snake) and cut into pieces weighing approximately 2 ounces (56 grams) each.
Proof:	To full proof (full expansion) at 104-108°F (40-42°C) and 85% relative humidity.
Bake:	15 to 17 minutes at 400°F (205°C).

Formula 31
Cinnamon Sugar

Grams	Ingredients	Mixing Instructions
600	Granulated Sugar	Blend thoroughly at
180	Korintje Cinnamon	low speed.
20	Vegetable Oil	
800	**Total Weight**	

Mixer: Vertical mixer with bowl and flat paddle agitator.
Note: The vegetable oil is used only to reduce dust during blending and application.
Application rate: 5 to 6% of the dough weight.

Note: Adherence of cinnamon sugar mix to dough can be enhanced by brushing a fine coating of vegetable oil or melted margarine (about 1% of dough weight) onto dough surface before the application of the dry mix.

Preconditioned raisins may be used at the rate of 5% of the dough weight by dispersing them over the area covered with the cinnamon-sugar mix.

Formula 32
Cinnamon Smear
(Cinnamon Roll Filling)

Grams	Ingredients	Mixing Instructions
225	1) Granulated Sugar	1) Blend sugar and cin-
225	Korintje Cinnamon	namon thoroughly.
1000	2) Brown Sugar	2) Add and blend the
200	Nonfat Dry Milk	ingredients thor-
800	Baker's Margarine	oughly at low speed.
200	3) Liquid Egg Whites	3) Add and mix smooth.
2650	**Total Weight**	

Mixer: Vertical mixer with bowl and flat paddle agitator.

Note: Do not aerate this filling. Mix at low speed only. Keep filling refrigerated until it is used.
Application Rate: 10 to 12% of the dough weight.

Formula 33
Melt-Away Filling
(For Sweet Rolls)

Grams	Ingredients	Mixing Instructions
750 150	1) Light Cake Crumbs Baker's Margarine	1) Blend ingredients thoroughly until a smooth paste is obtained.
160 90 60	2) Bread Flour Liquid Whole Eggs Vanilla Flavoring	2) Add ingredients and mix until thoroughly incorporated.
750 300	3) Granulated Sugar Vegetable Shortening	3) Add and mix until smooth.
230	4) Vegetable Oil	4) Add and mix smooth.
2490	**Total Weight**	

Mixer: Vertical mixer with bowl and flat paddle agitator.

Note: Keep filling refrigerated until it is used. To improve the spreadability of this filling, add more vegetable oil or more liquid whole eggs. Do not add water.

Application Rate: 10-15% of dough weight.

Note: This is an excellent filling for sweet rolls to be topped after proofing with a cheese or fruit topping.

Formula 34
Pecan Crunch Filling

Grams	Ingredients	Mixing Instructions
600	1) Dark Cake Crumbs	1) Break up crumbs.
1500	2) Granulated Sugar	2) Add. Blend well
450	Table Margarine	at low speed.
300	3) Bread Flour	3) Add. Mix smooth
60	Dried Whole Eggs	at low speed.
10	Salt	
112	Cinnamon	
28	Vanilla	
600	Invert Sugar	
1500	4) Pecan Meal	4) Add and incorporate.
750	5) Water (variable)	5) Add and mix smooth.
5910	**Total Weight**	

Mixer: Vertical mixer with bowl and flat paddle agitator.
Note: Keep filling refrigerated until it is used.
Application Rate: 20-25% of dough weight.
Note: This is an excellent filling for sweet rolls and coffee cakes in combination with *Cinnamon Crunch Topping.* (Formula 40)

Formula 35
Walnut Filling
(For Coffee Cakes)

Grams	Ingredients	Mixing Instructions
175	1) Table Grade Margarine	1) Blend thoroughly.
900	Light Cake Crumbs	
320	2) Bread Flour	2) Add ingredients and
660	Granulated Sugar	incorporate into
35	Cinnamon	the mix.
900	3) Walnut Pieces, Med.	3) Add and incorporate.
2990	**Total Weight**	

Mixer: Vertical mixer with bowl and pastry knife mixing attachment.
Note: This is a dry filling and it must be crumbly! It is a good and tasty filling to be rolled into the dough in conjunction with *Cinnamon Smear* (Formula 32) for a "split snake" make-up.
Application Rate:
   Cinnamon Smear: 12% of dough weight
   Walnut Filling: 15% of dough weight

Formula 36
Almond Filling

Grams	Ingredients	Mixing Instructions
900 600 100	1) Almond Paste Granulated Sugar Water	1) Blend ingredients until smooth and free of lumps.
800 3	2) Light Cake Crumbs Salt	2) Add and mix until smooth.
340	3) Liquid Egg Whites	3) Add and thoroughly incorporate into the filling.
2743	**Total Weight**	

Mixer: Vertical mixer with bowl and flat paddle agitator.
Note: Keep filling refrigerated until it is used!
Note: The almond paste may be totally or partially replaced with macaroon or kernel paste in this formulation. This requires a change in labeling.
Application Rate: 20-25% of dough weight.
Note: This filling is excellent for coffee cakes and fruit-topped sweet rolls.

Formula 37
Sweet Roll Icing

Grams	Ingredients	Mixing Directions
	Boiled Syrup:	
120 50 300	1) Granulated Sugar Icing Stabilizer* Water (75°F, 24°C)	1) Dry-blend sugar with stabilizer and disperse in water. Bring to a full boil for 3 minutes.
3 60	2) Salt Vegetable Shortening	2) Add salt and shortening to syrup and incorporate.
	Icing:	
1000	3) Powdered Sugar	3) Add half of the hot syrup to the sugar and mix smooth. Gradually add and incorporate the remainder of the syrup and mix smooth. Scrape bowl and beater intermittently.
1533	**Total weight**	

Note: Use this icing at 110-120°F (43-49°C) and apply to sweet rolls and coffee cakes about 10 minutes or later after baking.
* Commercial icing stabilizer containing agar and other vegetable gums. Use at level recommended by the manufacturer.
Note: Plastic shortening is added to icing to reduce brittleness and to prevent icing from "flaking off" or "chipping," i.e. falling off the product. Shortening may be replaced with hard fat flakes in warm climates.

Formula 38
Golden Streusel

Grams		Ingredients	Mixing Instructions
500	1)	Baker's Margarine	1) Blend thoroughly.
4		Liquid Egg Color	
6		Lemon Emulsion	
500	2)	Granulated Sugar	2) Add and incorporate.
1000	3)	Pastry Flour	3) Add and incorporate.
2010		**Total Weight**	

Mixer: Vertical mixer with bowl and pastry knife mixing attachment (a flat paddle mixing agitator may be used in place of the pastry knife, but may require more careful mixing).
Note: Do not overmix! The streusel must be dry to feel and must be easy to spread!
The mix may be rubbed through a screen with 1/4 inch (6.2 millimeter) openings.
Keep the ingredients and the streusel cool to prevent clumping!

Formula 39
Melt-Away Streusel

Grams	Ingredients	Mixing Instructions
600	1) Baker's Margarine	1) Blend thoroughly.
2.5	Liquid Egg Color	
2.5	Vanilla Flavoring	
750	2) Bread Flour	2) Incorporate into mar-
500	Powdered Sugar	garine.
1855	**Total Amount**	

Mix: Vertical mixer with bowl and pastry knife mixing attachment (a flat paddle mixing agitator may be used in place of the pastry knife, but may require more careful mixing).

Note: Do not overmix. Streusel should still contain small lumps of margarine which will melt into the product during baking. If properly mixed, this topping does not need to be rubbed through a screen.

Store this streusel in a cool environment.

Note: This streusel is not suitable for machine application!

Formula 40
Cinnamon Crunch Topping

Grams		Ingredients	Mixing Instructions
600	1)	Baker's Margarine	1) Mix smooth! Do not aerate!
1000	2)	Granulated Sugar	2) Add and incorporate ingredients into margarine. Mix until mass becomes crumbly.
725		Pastry Flour	
50		Cinnamon	
5		Vanilla Flavoring	
2380		**Total Amount**	

Mixer: Vertical mixer with bowl and pastry knife mixing attachment (a flat paddle mixing agitator may be used in place of the pastry knife, but may require more careful mixing).
Note: Do not overmix this topping!

APPENDIX

A

Baker's Percent

Baker's percent is a unique concept for formulating products and comparing formulations of different doughs and batters. Baker's percent relates the quantities of all ingredients to the total amount of flour or some other major ingredient in the formula. This is equivalent to saying that to every 100 pound (lb.) bag of flour, the baker adds 60 lb. (60%) water and 2 lb. (2%) salt. In order to indicate that the percentages relate to the total flour weight in the formula, the baker often identifies this relationship as "flour basis" (f.b.). Thus the 60 lb. water added per 100 lb. bag of flour in the mixing bowl is expressed as 60% (f.b.).

Sometimes, this relationship to flour is also described as "based on the total weight of flour in the formula equals 100%." If the formula calls for 72 lb. flour and 1.44 lb. (1 lb., 7 ounces) salt, then the percentage of salt is:

$$(1.44 \text{ lb.} \div 72 \text{ lb.}) \times 100\% \text{ (f.b.)} = 2\% \text{ (f.b.)}$$

The advantage of using "baker's percent" lies in the fact that a change in the amount of any ingredient, except in the base (flour), will affect only the percentage of this individual ingredient. The percentages of all other ingredients will remain constant. Also, since the amounts of all ingredients are expressed relative to the total amount of flour in the formula, it is easy to compare different formulations.

Even though the majority of bakers now use "baker's percent," formulations based on one gallon of water can still be found. Many formulations were once written as one or two gallon doughs. Here, the baker added sufficient flour to the specified amount of water to form a dough of his liking. All other ingredients remained constant. This method was generally used before bakers had scales to weigh their ingredients. It was based on volume measurements, similar to the methods still used by many home bakers.

Another measure for determining a batch size which is no longer commonly used is the *barrel of flour* (bbl), which equates to 196 lb. flour. Although few formulas utilized this weight measure for flour, the volume measure of one barrel (31.5 gallons) was at one time widely used for rating the capacity of mechanical mixers, such as a "2 bbl mixer." Bread dough mixers, however, are now rated according to the total amount of dough they are capable of mixing at one time. Only the size of vertical mixers is still rated according to the liquid volume capacity of the mixing bowl, e.g., "80 quart mixer."

APPENDIX

B

Sample Score Sheet

TABLE

BREAD EVALUATION

Date Mixed:			Date Scored:			
BREAD TYPE:			Age of Bread: Day(s)			
EXPERIMENTAL VARIABLE:						
PROJECT #:						
		BREAD SCORES				
BREAD						
QUALITIES	MAX SCORE					
EXTERNAL:	**30**					
Volume	10					
Symmetry	5					
Crust Color	10					
Break & Shred	5					
Descriptor Notations						
CRUMB STRUCTURE:	**35**					
Grain	15					
Texture	15					
Crumb Color	5					
Descriptor Notations						
SENSORY:	**35**					
Aroma	10					
Taste	15					
Mouthfeel	10					
Descriptor Notations						
TOTAL SCORE	**100**					
Absorption: %						
Mix Time: min/med. speed						
Proof Height: mm						
Proof Time: minutes						
Specific Volume: cm^3/g						
Volume: cm^3						
REMARKS						

CAKE EVALUATION

Date Baked: _____   Date Scored: _____

CAKE TYPE:		PROJECT:			
SCALING WEIGHT:		PAN TYPE:			
EXPERIMENTAL VARIABLE:					

CAKE SCORES					
SAMPLE NUMBER					
QUALITIES	MAX SCORE				
EXTERNAL:	**30**				
Volume	10				
Symmetry	5				
Crust Color	10				
Crust Character	5				
Descriptor Notations					
INTERNAL:	**35**				
Grain	10				
Texture	15				
Crumb Color	10				
Descriptor Notations					
SENSORY:	**35**				
Aroma	10				
Taste	15				
Mouthfeel	10				
Descriptor Notations					
TOTAL SCORE	**100**				
Baking Time: minutes					
Specific Volume: cm^3/g					
Crumb pH (24 Hours)					
REMARKS					

Quality Descriptors

Descriptors for Bread Evaluation

Volume:
01 Excessive
02 Too small

Symmetry:
11 Flat top
12 Bulging top
13 Peaked
14 Blisters, trace
15 Blisters, slight
16 Blisters, moderate
17 Blisters, severe
18 Low ends

Crust Color:
21 Too light
22 Speckled, spotty
23 Blotched, non-uniform
24 Too dark
25 Fish eye blisters

Break & Shred:
31 Lack of break & shred
32 Break on both sides
33 Uneven break, wild
34 Insufficient shred
35 Excessive shred

Crumb Grain:
41 Open, irregular
42 Tight
43 Small holes
44 Medium holes
45 Large holes
46 Thick cell walls
47 Collapsed cells

Crumb Texture:
51 Coarse, harsh
52 Weak crumb structure
53 Dry
54 Wet, tacky

Crumb Color:
61 Gray
62 Yellow
63 Tan
64 Light brown
65 Medium brown
66 Dark brown
67 Off-color
68 Slightly dark

Aroma:
71 Lack of aroma
72 Strong fermentation
73 Foreign aroma

Taste:
81 Strong fermentation
82 Sour
83 Too sweet
84 Not sweet enough
85 Salty
86 Bland
87 Bitter
88 Chemical
89 Nutty
90 Wheaty

Mouthfeel:
91 Dry
92 Slightly gummy
93 Gummy
94 Tough, chewy
95 Crumbly
96 Soft

Note: All descriptors can be adapted to individual requirements.

Descriptors for Bun Evaluation

Volume:
01 Excessive
02 Too small

Symmetry:
11 Non-uniform
    rise
12 Flat top
13 Excessive
    spread
14 Too little spread
15 Rounded

Crust Color:
21 Too light
22 Speckled, spotty
23 Blotched, non-
    uniform
24 Too dark
25 Fish-eye blisters

Shred:
31 No shred
32 Slight break
33 Severe break

Crust Character:
36 Rough, coarse
37 Blistered
38 Wrinkled

Crumb Grain:
41 Open, irregular
42 Tight
43 Small holes
44 Medium holes
45 Large holes
46 Thick cell walls

Crumb Texture:
51 Coarse, harsh
52 Weak crumb
    structure
53 Crumbly
54 Dry
55 Wet, tacky

Crumb Color:
61 Gray
62 Yellow
63 Tan
64 Light brown
65 Medium brown
66 Dark brown
67 Off-color
68 Slightly dark

Aroma:
71 Lack of aroma
72 Strong fermen-
    tation
73 Foreign aroma

Taste:
81 Strong fermen-
    tation
82 Sour
83 Too sweet
84 Not sweet
    enough
85 Salty
86 Bland
87 Bitter
88 Chemical

Mouthfeel:
91 Dry
92 Slightly gummy
93 Gummy
94 Tough, chewy
95 Crumbly

Descriptors for Cake Evaluation

Volume:
01 Excessive
02 Too small

Symmetry:
11 Flat top
12 Peaked surface
13 Slight depression
14 Collapsed center, dip
15 Dimple
16 Non-uniform (crust not smooth)
17 Blisters

Crust Color:
21 Too light
22 Spotty
23 Too dark
24 Off-color
25 Grease ring

Crust Character:
31 Tough, leathery
32 Slightly tacky, sticky
33 Tacky, sticky
34 Crust separating from crumb
35 Dry
36 Cracks in center
37 Cracks near edge

Crumb Grain:
41 Open, irregular
42 Dense, collapsed
43 Firm core near bottom
44 Peripheral cracks near edge
45 Peripheral tunnels
46 Horizontal cracks near center .
47 Blow holes
48 Tight
49 Irregular

Crumb Texture:
51 Coarse, harsh
52 Weak crumb structure
53 Dry
54 Wet, tacky
55 Tough, rubbery

Crumb Color:
61 Gray
62 Tan
63 Light brown
64 Brown
65 Dark
66 Off-color

Aroma:
71 Lack of aroma
72 Foreign aroma
73 Grainy

Taste:
81 Aftertaste
82 Too sweet
83 Not sweet enough
84 Bland
85 Chemical, leavening
86 Bitter
87 Acidic

Mouthfeel:
91 Dry
92 Slightly gummy
93 Gummy
94 Tough, chewy
95 Crumbly
96

Descriptors for Cake Muffins

Volume:
01 Excessive
02 Too small

Symmetry:
11 Flat top
12 Crust not smooth
13 Cracked
14 Peak
15 Crown
16 Lack of spread
17 Good spread
18 Excessive spread

Crust Color:
21 Too light
22 Spotty
23 Too dark
24 Off-color

Crust Character:
31 Leathery
32 Dry
33 Sticky

Crumb Grain:
41 Open, irregular
42 Dense, collapsed
43 Firm core near bottom
44 Blow holes
45 Peripheral tunnels
46 Horizontal cracks near center
47 Big holes
48 Small holes

Crumb Texture:
51 Coarse, harsh
52 Weak crumb structure

Crumb Color:
61 Gray
62 Tan
63 Light brown
64 Brown
65 Dark
66 Off-color

Aroma:
71 Lack of aroma
72 Foreign aroma

Taste:
81 Aftertaste
82 Too sweet
83 Not sweet enough
84 Bland, no flavor
85 Chemical taste
86 Leavening taste

Mouthfeel:
91 Dry
92 Slightly gummy
93 Gummy, cohesiveness
94 Tough, chewy
95 Crumbly
96 Slightly coarse
97 Coarse

Index

A

acetic acid 123
acid salt 145, 146, 184
active dry yeast 76
air classification 139
Air Flowrator 164
Alberger salt 79, 80
alcohol 73, 84, 150
alligator cut 238
alpha-amylase 65, 90, 114, 120
Alveograph 58, 61
American Association of Cereal Chemists (AACC) 50
ammonium chloride 72, 108
ammonium sulfate 72, 108
Amylograph 66
applesauce 153, 154
aqueous dispersion 118
aroma 169
ascorbic acid 13, 64, 109, 110
ash 70
automated bakeries, 16
azodicarbonamide 64, 65, 109, 110, 111

B

bacterial amylase 120
bagels 90
bake-out loss 41

Baker Compressimeter 50
baking 41, 165, 203, 204
baking powder 138, 157
baking raisins 105
baking soda 138, 146, 149, 171
bananas 153, 154
batch size 176
batter 154
batter mixing 159
batter temperature 157
batter viscosity 154, 217
batter weight 175
benzoyl peroxide 67
berries 208
beta-amylase 114
beta-carotene 145, 178
beta-glucan 101
biurea 110
blackstrap molasses 91
bleached raisins 105
bleaching agent 65, 67
blending of ingredients 24, 160
blueberries 153
boiling point 246
bran 69, 101
bran fiber 99
brass 220
bread flour 52, 59, 68, 223
bread pans 38
break 10
bromelain 115

bronze 220
brown sugar 85, 92, 246
browning reaction 83
Brownulated Brand Brown
    Sugar 85
buffering effect 17
bulk fermentation 12, 13
butter 193, 194, 245
butter flavor 152, 153
butter oil 152
butter-lemon-vanilla 152
buttercream 190

C

cake baking 137
cake doughnut 214, 217, 218
cake emulsifier 157, 158,
    172, 176, 178, 180
cake flour 138, 139
cake icing 192
cake mixes 141, 154
cake muffins 208, 209
cake shortening
    141, 142, 146, 191, 195
cake staling 173
cake texture 169
cakes 138, 190
calcium 63, 148
calcium bromate 111
calcium carbonate 72
calcium dioxide 111, 112
calcium iodate 111
calcium propionate 122, 123
calcium silicate 82, 220
calcium sulfate 72, 108, 184
calorie reduced 98, 155
caramelization 84
carbonic acid 19, 73
carboxymethylcellulose 217
carotene 67, 178
carrots 153

casein 148, 177, 216
cell structure 53, 169, 170
cell wall material 99
cellulose 83, 217
cellulose fiber 99, 100
chemical buffer 18
chemical dough development
    13
chemical leavening
    138, 145, 157, 166, 169,
    177, 180
chlorinated cake flour
    155, 171, 201
chlorination 139
chlorine dioxide 64
chocolate 193
chocolate cake
    140, 148, 149, 171, 172,
    176
chocolate liquor 148, 176
cholesterol 95, 98, 142
Chorleywood method 13
cinnamon roll dough 225
cinnamon rolls 223, 224, 225
citrus flavors 152
clear flour 69
coating 217
coating sugar 219
cocoa 148, 150, 176, 193
cocoa butter fat 149
cocoa fudge base 193, 194
coconut 192
Code of Federal Regulations
    63
coffee cake make-up 232
coffee cakes
    224, 230, 241, 243, 245,
    246
complex carbohydrates
    83, 99
compressed yeast
    74, 75, 128

dough strengtheners 95, 116, 223
dough water absorption 103
doughnut flour 216
doughnut frying 219
doughnut machines 216
doughnut pyrophosphate 217
dried fruit 208
dry diastatic malt 90
dry molasses 92
dumbbell shape 33
dutched cocoa 149

E

egg 141
egg bread 98
egg coloring 145, 178
egg protein 170
egg shade 178
egg wash 241
egg whites 142, 144, 184
egg yolk 142, 150
eggs 138
electric ovens 42
emulsified shortening 155
emulsifier 116, 139, 141, 142, 158
encapsulated salt 81
endosperm 69
environmental cabinet 45, 49, 173
enzyme activated wheat gluten 103
enzyme columns 88
enzyme-active soy flour 115
enzymes 87, 109, 110, 113, 115, 118, 120, 127
ethnic breads 97
ethoxylated monoglycerides 117, 127

ethyl vanillin 151, 152
experimental bakery 2
experimental baking 1, 3, 8, 11, 46, 127
extracts 150
eye appeal 46

F

Falling Number instrument 66
Farinograph 23, 58
fat absorption 216, 218, 219
fat replacement 155
fats 94
Fehling solution 83
fermentable sugar 73
fermentation 12, 16, 17, 19, 20, 21, 25
fiber 83
fillings 243, 244
filtering 220
filtering compound 220
finishing 161
flaked salt 79
flavors 150, 246
floor time 14, 25
flour 51, 52, 138, 245
flour additives 62
flour extraction 68
flour improvers 63
flour oxidants 20
flour quality 52
flour separation 69
foaming 220
folic acid 63
fondant 194
food coloring 192
formulations 180
French bread 90
frozen eggs 144
fructose 82, 84, 88, 93, 194

R

rack ovens 10
raisin bread 106
raisin juice concentrate 124
raisins 104, 107, 124, 153
raisins, conditioning 106
rapeseed 44
record keeping 3
reducing agents 112, 113
reducing sugar 83, 170, 177
reduction in calories 98, 155
reel ovens 41
refiners syrup 91
retarding 224
Rheograph 58, 62
rheological test 23
rolls 246
room temperature stable
    whole eggs 144
rope 122
rotor 162, 163, 164
rounders 9
rounding of dough 31

S

salmonella 144
salt 51, 78, 146, 147
sample size 6
San Francisco sour bread 73
sanitation 122
scissor cut 232
scoring 46
scoring cakes 168
shelf-life
    13, 14, 104, 121, 127,
    142, 154, 156, 209
shelf-life evaluation 45, 49,
    173

shelf-life test 49
short patent flour 139
shortening
    143, 145, 157, 158, 159,
    160, 176, 177, 84, 190, 191,
    193
shorts 69
shred 10, 37
single-layer cakes 177
slurry 162, 163, 164
snack cakes 148, 152, 195
snails 228
soaps 220
sodium acid pyrophosphate
    28, 146, 184
sodium aluminum sulfate
    146
sodium bicarbonate
    138, 145, 146
sodium diacetate 123
sodium lauryl sulfate 144
sodium silicoaluminate 82
sodium stearoyl lactylate 20
soluble fiber 101
sorbic acid 123
sorbitan monostearate
    142, 157, 178
soybean oil 95, 141
soyflour 96
specific gravity
    158, 159, 161, 162, 164, 165,
    191, 192, 193, 195, 203
specific volume 44, 168, 169
spices 153, 246
sponge cake 141, 143, 178
sponge dough 14
sponge temperature 16
spot-iced 230
spring wheat 52, 71
"sprinkles" 192
sprout damaged wheat 66

staling 119
starch 83
starch retrogradation
46, 119, 120
stearoyl lactylate 117, 127
straight dough 12, 225
straight dough method 11,
27, 223
straight grade flour 69,70
strawberries 153
streusel 230, 245, 246
succinylated monoglyceride
117
sucrose 82, 83, 84
sugar 82, 115,
138, 139, 155, 177, 184,
216, 217
sugar spots
86, 140, 146, 177
sulfhydryl group 110
sulfur dioxide 105
sweet dough 222, 224, 238
sweet roll icing 241
sweet rolls 225, 228, 230
swirl-iced 230
symmetry 169

T

tapioca starch 154
tartaric acid 104, 107, 124
taste 169
taste panel 4, 6, 173
tempering 141
templates 38
test baking 37, 137
testing parameters 173
test, significance 5
thermal death point 66
toasting 119
traveling tray oven 167
triangle test 5

tricalcium phosphate 82
triethyl citrate 144
trisaccharides 93
turbo milling 139, 140
Tweedy mixer 13

U

under-emulsification 158

V

vanilla 150
vanilla extract 151
Vanilla-Vanillin 151
vanillin 151, 152
variety breads 85
vegetable oil 127, 150, 219
vegetable shortening 95
vegetables 150, 153
vinegar 123
vital wheat gluten
70, 71, 100, 101, 102,
103
vitamins 62, 65, 81, 93
Volumeter 43, 168

W

water 51, 71, 138, 147
water absorption
23, 59, 96, 100, 111
water activity 217, 246
water brew 18, 19, 21
wedding cake 184
wet bulb temperature 40
wheat bread 71
wheat germ 69
wheat gluten 51
whey 96, 97, 148, 177
whey protein concentrates
148
whey solids 170

whipping agent 144
white layer cakes
   141, 152, 170, 179, 184
white pan bread 10, 41
white spots 203
whole eggs
   97, 98, 142, 143, 170, 178,
   184
whole wheat bread 70,
   71, 103, 122,
wild yeast 73, 92
winter wheat 52
wooden bench top ·28

X

xanthan gum 217
xanthophyll 67

Y

yeast 15, 40, 45, 51, 72,
   88, 89, 109,121, 122, 123,
   124, 222
yeast activity 78
yeast vitality 75
yellow layer cake 178
yellow prussiate of soda 80,
   182
yellow sponge cake 179

Z

Zante currants 105
zucchinis 153
zymase enzyme system 84